The Basque Children in Britain

The Basque Children in Britain

Committees, Colonies and Concerts

Yolanda Powell

Design by Chomp Creative Limited

ISBN 978-1-9999224-2-9

This book is dedicated to the memory of my mother
Alicia Pedrero Alberdi

Born 14 February 1925 in Gallarta, Vizcaya, Spain

Died 19 March 1995 in London, England

CONTENTS

List of Illustrations

Introduction

In 1967, a group of middle-aged men and women came together with their families to mark the thirtieth anniversary of their escape from the horrors of civil war in Spain to the relative calm of a campsite in southern England. Expecting to stay in Britain for at most three months, these Basque children – los niños vascos - had never returned to live in their home country. My mother was one of them.

Reunions of the Basque children became a regular affair and I was lucky enough to attend a number of these joyful, emotional get-togethers. Tears and laughter punctuated everybody's conversations. Sometimes, a song would start at one table and gradually be taken up by everyone present. Always, there was this sense of a special bond that tied together these men and women as closely if not more closely than the blood-ties of family.

Inspired by the reminiscences of my mother and of some of her friends, I resolved to write the story of their evacuation, which I began in the mid 1970s, after graduating from Oxford.

I talked at length with Wilfrid Roberts, who had been one of the driving forces behind the evacuation and care of the children. He welcomed me to his home in Cumbria and gave me access to a wealth of material, including committee meeting minutes, telegrams and letters. By then a man in his seventies, he was a terrifying driver but charming and flirtatious, and delighted that someone had decided to write about the Basque children.

I spoke to others who had been intimately involved in the running of homes for the evacuees. These included, in particular, Ronald Thackrah, who chaired the Basque Children's Committee in the 1940s, and Poppy Vulliamy, who had been especially involved in overseeing teenage boys. Walter Leonard, who took over from Poppy the care of the older Basque boys, came to see me and I visited Ramon Nadal, who adopted two Basque boys.

A number of Basque children filled in questionnaires for me and some agreed to be interviewed on tape to tell me their stories of how they came to England and of their experiences.

My research also took me to Friends House in London to consult back numbers of the Quaker newspaper, *The Friend,* and to the Foreign Office, where Gill Bennett, who subsequently became Chief Historian to the Foreign Office, kindly gave me access to the archives.

Some years after I first started on this work, a couple of other authors published notable works on the Basque child refugees. Dorothy Legarreta, an American academic, came to see me for help in her researches on the evacuation of the Basque children to England. In 1984, she published *The Guernica Generation*, a detailed study of the evacuation of Basque children not only to England but also to France, Belgium and the Soviet Union. In 1996, Adrian Bell published *Only for Three Months*, concentrating predominantly on the children who came to England and drawing on interviews with many of the people I had also interviewed some years before. More recently, Natalia Benjamin edited two volumes of Basque children's memories in 2007 and 2012.

In this book, I have included much detail on the workings of the organisations that looked after the children. Perhaps ironically, although I started out to write the story of the children, I found myself becoming more and more interested in the problems facing the British volunteers who brought them over.

It seems fitting to publish this account, at long last, in the year of the 85th anniversary of the children's evacuation.

Nowadays, the Basque children's reunions are primarily a means for the families of the niños to remember their story and exchange what we know about our parents' or grandparents' experiences. There are only a few niños still alive and, of those, not all are able to attend the reunion lunch, held in London as close as possible to 22 May - the date of the niños' arrival at Southampton Water.

My thanks go to all those who helped me in my researches, especially the Basque children, most notably Amador Diaz, Valentin Fernandez Osaba, Fausto Garcia and Rosa Garcia, Helvecia Hidalgo, Merche Jarero, Pedro Lopez, Laureana Puerta, Alicia Radcliffe-Genge, Rosa San Jose, Luis Sanz, Isabel Segurola, Juanita Vaquer. I hope their memory can live on, albeit in a small way, in this book.

Yolanda Powell
October 2022

Chapter One

Birth of the National Joint Committee

'We have come to the conclusion that the evacuation of as large a part of the civil population as possible is an urgent necessity.'

(Report on the visit by an all-party group of MPs to Spain in November 1936)

When civil war erupted in Spain in July 1936, public opinion throughout Europe was fiercely divided between supporters of the Republican government and those of the Nationalists. Atrocities on both sides were widely reported and distinguishing between truth and propaganda was as difficult then as it was in the 1990s in Bosnia or in 2022 in Ukraine.

In November 1936, a group of MPs from the House of Commons decided to try and find out for themselves what conditions were really like in Spain. They also wished to investigate stories of the torture and murder of prisoners in territories held by the Republican Government and which had been adversely reported on in the British press.

The Group was an all-party affair - three Unionist MPs, two Labour and one Liberal. They arrived in Barcelona on 22 November, when they witnessed a large demonstration sparked by the death three days previously of Durruti, a leading anarchist who before the Civil War had engaged in terrorist activities and whom the Group categorised in its final report as 'a capable and popular leader of the militia.' The MPs then went to Valencia on the south-eastern Mediterranean coast where the Republican government had set up its headquarters. The MPs met a number of important ministers, including Del Vayo, the Foreign Minister, and Irujo, the 'Catholic Basque'.

El ministro de Estado, Sr. Alvarez del Vayo, ha ofrecido un almuerzo, en Valencia, a los parlamentarios ingleses que realizan su misión de observadores neutrales en España. (Foto L. Vidal.)

Fig 1. Members of the Parliamentary Group with Alvarez del Vayo. (ABC, a left-wing Madrid daily)

The British politicians spent barely a day in Valencia before leaving for Madrid, where they were put up only one mile from the battlefront. From there they were able to observe the effects of air raids on the civilian population and the very great problems facing Madrid in having to deal with a continuous influx of refugees from the neighbouring region.

In the report published on their return from Spain, the MPs reviewed the political situation in Madrid, 'The Central Government, in spite of the difficulties with which it is faced, seems gradually to be gaining in prestige and authority', and the Junta then running the city comprised 'enthusiastic working-class lads mostly.'

The MPs were concerned about the fate of political prisoners, of whom some 14,000 were held in official prisons. The number was reducing as prisoners were taken away, either officially to another prison (but never reaching their destination) or by being seized by armed gangs. The prisoners remaining in the Madrid gaols were reported to be afraid of being released before Franco, a leading Nationalist general, took Madrid but equally afraid of the reprisals that might take place if Madrid fell when they were still in prison.

The MPs wrote to the Spanish Government about the fate of political prisoners and on 30 November they received a reply from Largo Caballero, the Prime Minister. He assured them that he would set up a Commission for Security to ensure better treatment and would allow the British chargé d'affaires in Madrid to review its results.

The Parliamentary Group was also deeply moved by the plight of the civilian population in Madrid, under threat from air raids and suffering serious shortages of food and fuel as only one road out of Madrid was clear, that to Valencia. After some consideration, the Group concluded that the evacuation of the civilian population was necessary. 'We have been informed that French organisations have undertaken the care of 50,000 children who are to be taken to France. English organisations might make a similar offer.'

The MPs sent several telegrams to Ministers in Britain. In the first, they urged on the Secretary of State for Foreign Affairs the evacuation and partial maintenance of women, children and non-combatants and in the second they asked that Parliament should vote monies for the evacuation of Embassy refugees, being honour bound to save British subjects.

The Group also sent an appeal jointly to Baldwin, the British Prime Minister, and Blum, the French Premier, for 'at least one thousand Frenchmen and one thousand Britons driving their own cars fully supplied with reserve petrol and ample food organised in columns to come to Madrid to assist in evacuation immediately. Suggest Royal Automobile Club and Automobile Association and Society of Friends organise British volunteers.'

Although nothing came of this appeal for a massive convoy, some members of the Parliamentary Group, on returning home, set up the National Joint Committee for Spanish Relief in December 1936. The committee was established on non-party lines to help co-ordinate relief work. Its first actions were to evacuate children from Madrid by lorries, which were subsequently used for food transport in Barcelona under the general direction of the Quakers. Other work included the setting up of colonies for refugees at Puigcerda in Catalonia and the sending of regular food and medical aid to Spain.

Throughout the civil war, the National Joint Committee was one of the most active of the organisations involved in supplying relief aid to the people of Spain. They would also play the most important part in persuading the British Government to allow the Basque children into the country.

Fig 2. Members of the National Joint Committee helping to load a lorry of supplies for Spain. The Earl of Listowel, Wilfrid Roberts, Ellen Wilkinson. (Private collection)

Chapter Two

Naval Protection, Blockades and other Official Problems

'The action of the non-intervention committee may be to precipitate the famine which is already threatening the lives of thousands of Spanish children.'

(Edith Pye to Viscount Cranborne, 21 February 1937)

From early 1937, there was a growing awareness of the problems facing the civilian population caught up in the Spanish war but proposals for evacuation of civilians or for relief aid were met initially with some suspicion by the Spanish Government. The Foreign Minister, Del Vayo, turned down a scheme of food aid proposed at Geneva in December 1936. In January 1937, Ogilvie Forbes, the British chargé d'affaires, cabled from Valencia, 'Spanish Government are at present opposed to evacuation of Spaniards from their territory. Under present conditions, appeal for evacuation can only be addressed to authorities where persons concerned are women, children or men above military age whose British origin or connection with business can be fully established.'

Despite these restrictions, Royal Navy ships were quite heavily involved in evacuating British and other subjects from Spain throughout the early months of 1937, though not without accusations of bias. Ogilvie Forbes wrote to Roberts, an official at the Foreign Office, 'Franco's friends have for obvious reasons had an advantage over this side in airing their griefs in London and Hendaye.' Hendaye was the place of residence of the British Ambassador, Sir Henry Chilton, whose pro-Nationalist leanings were well known. An incident on board a British ship at the end of February, when Polish evacuees were found to have incorrect papers, prompted Ogilvie Forbes to write, 'considerable feeling was expressed by the crowd of workers who collected at the landing stage and remarks were made to the effect that His Majesty's ships carried away enemies and never brought back friends.'

The Foreign Office did not welcome the involvement of the Navy in this work and endeavoured to limit as far as possible the circumstances under which it could be carried out - 'it will in any case no longer be possible for HM's ships to evacuate Spanish and other foreign nationals except in small numbers and in exceptionally deserving circumstances and in the course of the normal routine duties of those ships.' (Telegram 18 March to Ogilvie Forbes)

A major concern of the British government was to uphold the doctrine of non-intervention - not interfering on either side in the civil war. This created problems when ships might have to run Nationalist blockades to get through to ports since, 'blockade is undoubtedly one of the insurgents' most powerful weapons' (Cranborne to David Grenfell MP). The Foreign Office agreed, however, to approach the insurgent authorities concerning individual ships that were taking provisions to be distributed by one of the British relief organisations 'known to be working impartially for the relief of the civilian population on both sides.'

This question of impartiality was a problem for the National Joint Committee in its dealings with officials. Many of the latter believed that the National Joint Committee was too partisan in support of the Republican government and favoured instead the work of another umbrella organisation, the General Relief Fund for Distressed Women and Children in Spain. A key factor in official thinking was the League of Nations report *Relief of Distress in Spain* published in January 1937.

The Report gave a brief history of the founding of the National Joint Committee soon after Christmas 1936 which, it said, was largely due to the initiative of Wilfrid Roberts MP, the Liberal member of the Parliamentary Mission to Spain. The National Joint Committee had at first proposed to co-ordinate the activities of all the British relief societies in Spain. Sir Edward Grigg MP, representing the General Fund, had suggested that the Fund co-operate in establishing a clearing-house for information. This was opposed by the left-wing members of the National Joint Committee and, therefore, the General Fund was not represented. Some friction arose thereafter between the two organisations over such things as the timing of appeals for funds. Other than the Society of Friends and the Save the Children Union, the agencies represented on the National Joint Committee were seen by the authors of the report as primarily left-wing.

Conversely, the General Fund was seen as less partisan, with representatives from all churches and prominent people in party political organisations. The General Fund Committee had, moreover, decided it could not help organisations that used political arguments in their appeals.

The conclusion of the Foreign Office was that the General Fund was the 'only one of the two which is strictly impartial'.

The early date of issue of the report, barely a month after the founding of the National Joint Committee, and the relative prominence of those involved on the General Fund may well indicate that a kind of establishment bias existed against the National Joint Committee from its very beginnings.

Members of the National Joint Committee were lobbying the Government from early on in 1937 to try and do something positive to help alleviate the distress in Spain. On 21 February, Edith Pye, a well-known Quaker and member of the National Joint Committee, wrote to Lord Cranbourne questioning the wisdom of allowing German and Italian warships to police the Spanish coast from Malaga to the French frontier (which they did under the terms of the non-intervention pact). 'Such control,' she wrote, 'by Germany and Italy alone might have the power to hamper the entry of food into these ports and, thus, the action of the non-intervention committee may be to precipitate the famine which is already seriously threatening the lives of thousands of

Spanish children.'

During the same month, David Grenfell and Wilfrid Roberts had gone to see Lord Cranbourne, in the company of Professor Catlin, to urge a 'great international humanitarian effort' to ease the famine conditions in Spain.

The Foreign Office, however, soon had to face lobbying not merely from the likes of the National Joint Committee but also from its own officials stationed in Spain. Sir Henry Chilton, the British Ambassador to Spain, sent on to the Secretary of State, Anthony Eden, a communiqué from Bates, his Consul at Santander. In his note, Bates underlined the ineffectiveness of the supposed insurgent blockade of Santander, pointing out that the port authorities were sweeping the port area and entrance channel twice daily as well as covering the area by seaplane searches when weather permitted. No mines had been found and, since the beginning of February, vessels, including three British, had been entering quite safely.

The intention behind Bates's communiqué was to see whether the British Navy could not assist in the evacuation of some of the hundreds of people trying to leave Spain from the North, including, according to Bates, '156 Cubans, 100 Mexicans, 25 Argentinians, 10 French, 4 Belgians, 3 Peruvians, 5 Swiss, 10 Americans and about 1000 Spaniards.'

Bates' argument that it was safe for ships to enter at Santander was generally supported by Sir Henry Chilton who added that Stevenson, the Consul in Bilbao, had informed him of the entry of some two hundred vessels into Bilbao, which was also supposed to have been mined by the insurgents. No British ships had entered, however, for some six weeks. In view of the impending insurgent offensive expected in the North, Chilton urged that 'in the next few weeks HM ships should develop the utmost possible activity in humanitarian work and should make every possible endeavour to remove from Bilbao and Santander all those who are now waiting with permits to leave.'

Such humanitarian impulses were not mirrored in the Foreign Office. Pollock, the desk officer receiving the communications, minuted to his fellow civil servant, Gloyne Cox, 'grateful if you would give this despatch consideration, before definitely turning down the scheme.' Gloyne Cox obliged, expressing concern at the possible loss of British destroyers but putting forward no clear reason why these should be at particular risk, commenting that HM Navy was already overworked and that the other countries concerned should take care of their own nationals. Finally, Gloyne Cox noted that if merchant vessels were moving in and out of the ports, local arrangements for shipping out evacuees ought to be possible.

At about the same time as Bates was putting forward his views on the desirability of evacuating adults, the Basque Government was formulating proposals for the large-scale evacuation of Basque children and seeking assurances of British protection for a steamer to take the children to France. Sir Henry Chilton sent a telegram to the Foreign Office on 12 March stating that he intended to inform the insurgent authorities of the plan and raising the possibility that the ship carry an insurgent naval officer 'to observe the strict correctness of our actions.' A letter from Chilton of 6 March possibly arrived at the same time, suggesting that the General Relief Fund enquire about vessels.

Pollock wrote to John Parks of the General Relief Fund Committee and Mrs Miller of the National Joint Committee on 13 March but was not positive about the scheme. He pointed out that mines were less danger to merchant ships than to destroyers and that HM ships were precluded from entering the ports. The suggestion was put forward 'for what it is worth.' The General Relief Fund Committee saw the scheme in the same light, 'as you say, there are many objections to the scheme and I very much fear it may be impracticable.'

Notwithstanding the lack of response from London, Chilton advised on 26 March that evacuation arrangements had been agreed by the insurgents and that the children would be evacuated by 3 April.

Despite the evident reluctance of officials in London for the Navy to be involved in evacuation work, it managed to play an important role in the transportation and safeguarding of a substantial number of refugees. By early April, the Government was able to reply to a Parliamentary Question from David Grenfell to the effect that HM ships had transported in total some 17,000 Spaniards and others from ports on the north coast of Spain, some three hundred refugees had been evacuated from the Chilean Embassy in Madrid to Marseilles by way of Valencia and 450 children evacuated to St Jean de Luz from Bilbao by British destroyers.

On 8 April, Stevenson, the Consul at Bilbao, sent a long telegram to the Foreign Office which outlined a daring proposal to come from the hands of a government official. In collaboration with the French Consul, Stevenson had proposed to the Basque Government the evacuation of large numbers of women and children because of the dangers to the civilian population from air raids. The Basque Government was reported as eager for such a scheme and would issue passports regardless of politics (this last point was always an important principle to the British in dealing with such cases).

The proposal was to use two ships - the *Habana*, a cruise ship, and the *Goizeko Izarra*, a yacht - to be commissioned by the British and French navies with a skeleton crew only on board. Each ship could, it was thought, take 5,500 evacuees. The two vessels would have to be escorted by British and French men-of-war. It was estimated that some 15,000 women and children would be ready for immediate evacuation and the Basque Government had agreed that refugees could re-enter Spain anywhere they wished after their evacuation. Stevenson pointed out it would be necessary to consider the problem of refugees who might need to be cared for in France (or Britain) but who would have no means of support of their own. Furthermore, he wondered whether, in the event that commissioning of Spanish vessels were not possible, British or French Government ships might be used. The question was in his view of 'extreme urgency' and he asked for early consideration of the proposal.

The initial response in London was not encouraging. A draft reply drawn up on 9 April rejected the possibility of such massive evacuation. There was concern over who would pay and it was felt that General Franco's approval would be essential together with an undertaking that his forces would not interfere with the ships' passage. In the view of the official drafting the reply, if such assurances were forthcoming from Franco, then any ships could have their normal

Spanish crew. An escort was doubtful. It was suggested that the British and French consuls should be on board instead to satisfy any misgivings Franco might have. Further, the 'suggestion that some of the refugees should come to the UK should not be encouraged for the present.'

Sir Henry Chilton supported the view that Franco's agreement would be necessary and that the presence on board of the British and French Consuls should be sufficient guarantee. The Secretary of State, Eden, however, questioned the logic of risking the Consuls' lives in this way - 'What becomes of our warning? [that merchant ships would be entering Bilbao at their own risk]'.

Although Stevenson's cable of the 8th was worded as though the evacuation were his own initiative, a private letter sent by Stevenson to his Ambassador at Hendaye and forwarded by Chilton to Eden shows quite clearly that he was acting on the original instigation of the Basque Government. Herein probably lies the explanation why the officials in London did not express surprise at Stevenson's taking this somewhat unconventional approach. The extracts that Chilton forwarded to the Secretary of State show how clear was Stevenson's analysis of the conditions prevailing in the Basque country.

The first extract concerned the proposal for the evacuation of a significant number of civilians:

'On Wednesday morning I received a visit from Manuel de la Sota. He told me that his brother and other leading Basque Nationalists, both in and out of office, were much perturbed by the succession of air raids on civilian centres causing much loss of life and by their inability to check these owing to the superiority of their enemies. Could something be done about a large-scale evacuation of the women and children? We discussed this matter from many points of view and finally de la Sota agrees with me that such a job had best be tackled by both Great Britain and France. In the evening he came back with Casteran and Luisa, Secretary General of Gobernacion and, incidentally, a very good friend of Innes and myself. Well, the long telegram we sent you represents the gist of several hours talk, and several hours coding. Both Casteran and myself feel strongly that what is practicable should be done, as no doubt you and your French colleague feel also.'

'While the Basque Government are most agreeable to the Anglo-French proposal, I might as well say that the suggestion from de la Sota was officially inspired, so that we are really saving their face. This is perhaps a good thing as, if Salamanca [ie Franco] knew the facts, they might raise difficulties there. The Basques of course insist on their ships being escorted both ways and this is understandable. They agree to wash out all 'political clearance'.'

Other extracts dealt with the daily air raids and the approach of Eguia, the 'First Lord of the Basque Admiralty as we call him' to ask Stevenson to telegraph Chilton to enable a ship to be released from St Jean de Luz. Additionally, Eguia spoke of the difficulties between the Basque Government and the Spanish administration in Valencia:

'Eguia told me.... that it was the general belief of Basques in Government offices from the President down that Valencia's failure to send promised, adequate aircraft to enable Bilbao to ward off raiders, was really Valencia's policy to allow the independent Basques a dose of such punishment as they would not easily forget. Of course, if Valencia and Bilbao carry their private quarrels to such lengths, anything may happen, but it is difficult to believe in such an allegation against Largo Caballero and his cabinet, who, if the truth were known, probably have no aircraft to send. So far there have been no reprisals against prisoners. On the morning on which Durango was bombed Gobernacion had all political prisoners there, 6, I believe, immediately removed to Bilbao. The Basque Government was not going to leave the slightest chance to another massacre, possibly by Basque peasants who, after all, are also only human. You have heard of the frightfulness committed at Durango. Two hundred killed, two hundred wounded. Two churches destroyed burying worshippers while mass was being said.'

At the same time as Consul Stevenson was expressing his concern over the bombing of civilian populations, the Save the Children International Union was considering the possibility of evacuating children from the war zone. Mrs Small of the Union wrote two letters to Pollock, the first concerning a scheme to send a food boat to the Basque country, which could then be used to evacuate 100 Nationalist children, and the second relaying information from the Comité International de la Croix Rouge at Santander that the Basque Government wanted to send away children whose parents could not feed them 'pour la durée des hostilités'. In this connection it was estimated that about one hundred children would go to France and another hundred to Nationalist Spain.

Meanwhile, in Hendaye, Auguste Werner of the Union visited Sir Henry Chilton and explained to him the Union's proposal. Chilton explained to Werner that no guarantee of naval protection for a foodship could be given since Franco's policy was to starve Bilbao, Santander and Gijon into surrender; a policy which could be defeated through the distribution of food. In Chilton's view even the evacuation of insurgent children was unlikely to persuade Franco. Furthermore, the food would not be needed if Franco's forces gained entry.

Pollock replied to Mrs Small promptly, pointing out the costs that would be involved, even if the boat were free; the project 'should not be undertaken without the financial backing necessary for its successful execution.' By 15 April, the Union had decided that '(given) present situation around Bilbao we think it wiser to take no steps for the moment.'

The Foreign Office was still agonising over Stevenson's proposal. In correspondence with the Consul, the Foreign Office suggested that if the Basque Government were willing to make arrangements for ships manned by Basques and the French Government were prepared to receive the refugees, then His Majesty's Government would approach the insurgents to try and obtain an undertaking which would obviate the need for an escort. Furthermore, it was stated that the Basque Government should include political hostages among the numbers evacuated. This last suggestion was dismissed by Stevenson who pointed out that the insurgents had failed to accept a recent Basque offer for an exchange of prisoners but rather had continued to bomb the civilian population in Durango.

Clearly, the officials in London were most unwilling to involve the

Navy in any of the proposals being put forward at this time and equally keen to avoid any public expenditure on evacuations or subsequent care of refugees. They were reinforced in their determination to deter any such requests by the receipt of a secret Admiralty telegram of April 16, relayed from HMS Blanche, that the then current situation with reference to minelaying in north Spanish waters did not justify the use of destroyers to evacuate non-British refugees from ports in northern Spain. Ambassador Chilton agreed with this assessment and as far as London was concerned that should have marked the end of British naval involvement. The climate of opinion changed radically, however, after Guernica.

Chapter Three

Guernica

'I have decided to end the war rapidly in the North. If surrender is not immediate I shall raze Vizcaya to the ground.'

(General Mola, 27 March 1937)

Of all the atrocities committed during the Spanish Civil War, Guernica made most impact outside Spain at the time and is the one that most people remember today. The bombing of towns was not a new phenomenon, as witness the attacks on Durango, and, indeed, an editorial of 7 May 1937 in the Quakers' newspaper, *The Friend*, condemned the use of ruthless bombing of civilians, pointing out that it had been used already in outposts of the Empire. The outrage felt at the bombing of Guernica, however, with the loss of perhaps 1,600 lives, was exceptionally strong and due, in no small part, to the emotional and highly descriptive despatches from George Steer, a journalist working for *The Times*.

Interestingly, Steer attended several meetings of the National Joint Committee and used to report back on such matters as the conditions prevailing in Bilbao. Steer's articles on the bombing of Guernica, a market town and ancient capital of Euzkadi (the Basque country), appeared first in *The Times* on 27 April, the day after the bombing. The tone of Steer's articles is clear from this extract from the first one, the impact of which on British public opinion is not difficult to imagine:

'In the form of its execution and the scale of the destruction it wrought, no less than in the selection of its objective, the raid on Guernica is unparalleled in military history. Guernica was not a military objective. A factory producing war material lay outside the town and was untouched..... The object of the bombardment was seemingly the demoralisation of the civil population and the destruction of the cradle of the Basque race. Every fact bears out this appreciation, beginning with the day the deed was done. Monday was the customary market day in Guernica...'

Although Franco quickly tried to claim that Guernica was actually bombed and set fire by the Republicans, few people believed him. To the outside world it appeared quite clear that German pilots had bombed and machine-gunned an innocent civilian population for more than three hours. Guernica marked a change in attitudes towards the two sides fighting in the civil war, at least among some of the media - *Time*, *Life* and, later, *Newsweek*, thereafter supported the Republican side.

The bombing of Guernica (and Barcelona) coloured much of the early thinking at the beginning of the Second World War concerning the effects of large-scale air raids on civilian populations. Picasso's famous painting remains as powerful a symbol today of the horrors of war and fascism as when it was first executed. The important point about Guernica in the context of the Basque children was that in late April the climate of public opinion in Britain was now strongly in favour of doing something to help alleviate the distress of civilians caught up in the war.

The National Joint Committee was swift to seize the opportunity and on 27 April Wilfrid Roberts wrote to Pollock at the Foreign Office with a proposal to bring an unspecified number of children to England. He used the fact that France and Belgium had taken children already and that the Netherlands and Scandinavia had indicated that they were willing to do so as grounds for Britain's doing the same. In this first proposal, only children over nine years of age would be brought out, to be settled in groups of around fifty with some ultimately going to people who had applied for temporary adoption. The Basques were said to be ready to charter a ship and, once definite approval was given, an appeal for funds would be made. The proposal was referred to the Home Office.

On 28 April, the Spanish Ambassador in London asked the Secretary of State for Foreign Affairs, Eden, if the British Navy would give protection for Spanish ships transporting refugees to France. This was agreed to, provided the refugees were not chosen on the basis of their political position and that Stevenson could supervise the arrangements in Bilbao. Before Guernica the British Government had not been noticeably eager to help in evacuations but now it was evident that the only acceptable move from the viewpoint of domestic politics was to help in the evacuation of civilians. This stance was taken by the Government in spite of strong opposition by some its senior civil servants, notably Geoffrey Mounsey and Chilton.

A minute from Sir Geoffrey to Eden on 2 May shows unequivocally the Assistant Under Secretary's views. He quotes Sir Henry Chilton as having told him, 'there are observers waiting in Bilbao to find any pretext for showing that HMG are by their action there violating the terms of the non-intervention agreement'. His argument was that intervening in a region that was under military attack, helping food to reach a city under siege and assisting in the evacuation of the civilian population was 'just as effective as anything which has been done by the other foreign powers, against whose activities in Spain we have from time to time found it necessary to protest.' Mounsey's chilling conclusion was that it was 'perfectly open to the Basque Government to save these people, without any intervention by HMG, either by accepting General Franco's offer (of a neutral zone) or by surrendering.'

The arguments of officials were not enough compared with the outcry concerning indiscriminate bombing of civilians. Eden confirmed the Government's willingness to assist in evacuating civilians at Parliamentary Question Time on 3 May but added, on the subject of the possible evacuation of Basque children to England, that he understood no final arrangements had yet been made.

Ellen Wilkinson MP interjected that she had a telegram stating that four thousand children were ready to sail and asked whether the

Foreign Office was ready to admit them if appropriate arrangements were made. Eden refused to be drawn, commenting that his concern was with protection on the high seas.

The Cabinet on 5 May was concerned at the prospect of large numbers of children coming to England. The Minister of Health asked for information about the four thousand who were allegedly coming but Eden thought that any such arrival was unlikely. The First Lord of the Admiralty remarked that one suggestion was that the figure of four thousand was being used in order to stimulate subscriptions to the fund that had been set up for the purpose of bringing Basque children out of Bilbao.

Meanwhile, Guernica had already passed into the political vocabulary. At Question Time on 6 May, Sir Alexander Knox asked about the Nationalist suggestion of a neutral zone and stated that, in his view, Franco was 'just as humane as..........any sentimental supporter of the Spanish Government in this country.' Mr Mander was swift to rejoin, '…was not his attitude to the civil population very clearly indicated at Guernica?'

The fact that permission was ultimately given for Basque children to come to England was very largely credited afterwards to the impact Guernica had had on public attitudes. Certainly, Wilfrid Roberts wrote to Aguirre on 8 May in the following terms, 'I can assure you that the bombardment of Guernica and other towns and the machine gunning of civilians has shocked British public opinion very much indeed and there is a very widespread desire in my country to help you by accepting your refugee children.' Revealingly, he added, 'the most practical way of protesting is by giving hospitality to some of your brave people.' In other words, the reception of refugees was being seen here as quite clearly a political act.

George Steer, in his book *The Tree of Guernica*, published only a year afterwards, was convinced that Guernica had been the decisive factor:

'Popular feeling forced the Government of Great Britain to take two decisions: to admit 4,000 Basque children refugees to the United Kingdom, and to agree to protect all shipping, whether British, foreign or even Spanish, which was taking children, women and men past military age away from the horrors of Bilbao.'

Chapter Four

The Battle for 4000

'Home Secretary has prohibited entry children over 12 STOP Our Committee's representative Dr Ellis just returned from Bilbao says this and limitation to 2000 has caused consternation STOP Have telephoned Sir John'

(Duchess of Atholl in cable to Eden, 18 June 1937)

When the National Joint Committee first wrote to the Foreign and Home Offices asking leave to bring to England child evacuees from Bilbao, no mention was made of the number of children involved. The number depended on how many funds could be raised for their maintenance in England. Wilfrid Roberts pointed out in his letter of 27 April to Montague Pollock at the Foreign Office that he understood that the Basque Government already had lists of children who might be evacuated. More details would be furnished once the Committee had the go-ahead and also had a better idea of how much money could be raised.

Despite the vagueness of the Committee's application, it seems clear that initially the number of around 2,000 children was in their minds. Mrs Leah Manning, a forceful left-wing educationalist and former MP, was already in the Basque Country making arrangements for the evacuation. On 29 April, she cabled Wilfrid Roberts that doctors, nurses and teachers had been arranged for 2,000 children. However, the following day, Mrs Manning was cabling again that the

Basque Government was requesting a British passenger steamer for 4,000 children plus adults. A stream of correspondence followed over several days concerning the Basque Government's proposals to charter various ships and evacuate varying numbers of civilians, adults as well as children.

Of particular importance was a proposal relayed by Leah Manning on 2 May that some 2,300 children were to be evacuated to France by the Confédération Générale du Travail (CGT), the French labour organisation. According to her correspondence with Wilfrid Roberts, on hearing of this proposal she immediately cabled MPs and the Trades Union Congress asking them to follow the CGT example.

At this time, Azcarate, the Republican Ambassador in London, was supposed to be finding a ship for the evacuation of as many as 4,000. However, according to Roberts's reply to Mrs Manning, the Ambassador had not yet received instructions and was, moreover, in Paris at the time. Once the Basques in London did receive instructions, they found that the cost of chartering a suitable ship or ships was high - they found two at £700 per day, each capable of taking 1,500 passengers, but had to wire Bilbao before proceeding further.

Basques in France suggested that the *Habana* could take the children to England and Roberts asked Leah Manning's opinion on 5 May. Her reply was not encouraging - the *Habana* was in constant use for the evacuation of civilians, including the aged, to France. However, the next day (7 May) Mrs Manning wired Roberts again to say that consideration was being given to the *Habana* after all and that a decision would be made after a comparison of terms with the other ships. Medical examinations of the children were already taking place by then, although the National Joint Committee had still not received the go-ahead from the relevant ministries back home.

Mrs Manning was quite determined to get the maximum possible number of children to England and tended to ignore any advice to the contrary from England. She appears to have made promises to the Basque authorities that were not within her power to give and, having made them, stubbornly refused to accept any alternative outcome.

One of Mrs Manning's requests to Roberts at this time was to ask him whether Lord Nuffield might find a ship for the Asistencia Social to send children to Russia, which was willing to receive a large number. Wilfrid Roberts replied by letter (safe hand of Dr Ellis, one of the doctors who examined the potential evacuees) on 8 May, commenting in exasperated terms on the 'extraordinary rumour' that Lord Nuffield might charter a ship for Russia:

'I really feel it is the sort of rumour which does not help at all and, as you know, we are busy enough preventing the suggestion that the Basques are Reds and it seems to me that some unfriendly person has suggested it. If the Russians wish to have children, they are in a strong position to send a ship themselves.'

Throughout this correspondence, until 11 May no indication was given of the number of children who would be coming to England, although the National Joint Committee, in a letter to the Home Office of 10 May, indicated that the funds raised thus far and continuing to be raised should enable the Committee to deal with 2,000 children for six months. On 11 May, Roberts cabled Leah Manning with the clear information that homes were being prepared for 2,000 children although, in Roberts's opinion, the Government was making difficulties. £17,000 had been collected and the Roman Catholic authorities had undertaken to place 1,200 children. The official involvement of the Church was important since the Basque Nationalists wanted to be able to maintain 'the integrity of their children's Catholicism' by having the children go to Catholic colonies or private homes. Leah Manning's comment on this last is revealing, 'but all English Catholics are pro-Franco, that would be impossible.'

Mrs Manning was concerned by this time that the Consul, Stevenson, would not give authorisation for the embarkation of children till he received word from London. By 14 May, Leah Manning was becoming panicky – she sent four cables to Roberts alone, noting in one of them that she had also cabled prominent politicians. The *Habana*, which had been available for the children, had now had to be diverted to evacuating other people to France. Stevenson had refused the embarkation of the children and this was dismissed by Leah Manning as having been for a remarkably petty reason, 'Whitsun holiday ought not to be allowed interfere with a matter such urgency.' Stevenson's hands were, however, tied; he had as yet received no word from London.

While this first cable was winging its way to London, Roberts was busy despatching one to Mrs Manning. Here, at last, Roberts gives some indications of the British Government's requirements and the number of children likely to be approved. He emphasises that the Home Office is still hesitating and unlikely to approve more than 2,000. If the *Habana* can carry 4,000, he suggests, then it should be sent to Bordeaux first, dropping 2,000 off there and then coming on to Southampton (where a camp was being prepared). Authorisation for 2,000 was expected to reach Stevenson the following day. The Home Office requirements were that one adult woman accompany every 20 children, including a proportion of teachers. Children between the ages of six and 12 were to be preferred.

Leah Manning's reaction was swift and emotional. First, she emphasized that 4,000 had been selected a week ago, that they could have 10,000 with no problem and that the doctors (Ellis and Russell) were working from eight in the morning until midnight every day, interrupted frequently in their work by air raids. Second, she cabled that there was great anxiety because 4,000 had been promised evacuation (by whom, we wonder) and the government department responsible was working round the clock. Furthermore, a German pilot, 'captured yesterday declares intense bombardment Bilbao imminent.' Third, she repeated the urgent need for evacuation, claimed that the *Habana* was, in fact, still available (in direct contradiction to her earlier cable) but would be diverted unless the authorisation was given. Meanwhile, Bilbao was suffering from bombings night and day.

A reply from Roberts ignored Leah Manning's histrionics but concentrated on relaying the information that preparations were well advanced for a reception camp in Southampton and that the Basque delegation in Paris had agreed with the Bordeaux proposal. A major concern of the Ministry of Health appeared to be the possibility of overcrowding on the *Habana*.

The following day, Roberts confirmed that official sanction

had been given for 2,000 and no more - although he left open the possibility of permission's being granted for a further 2,000 at some later stage. The children had to arrive the following week and Stevenson had been instructed that they should be split between boys and girls in the proportion of 9:11, all between the ages of six and twelve years. One hundred adult female teachers and attendants and fifteen priests would be allowed to accompany the children. Each child, in turn, was required to have an identification disc bearing name, sex, date of birth, full names of parents, full names of next of kin, and last permanent address in Bilbao. (How large a disc would be required to carry all this information did not appear to have been considered.)

Wilfrid Roberts also sent a cable to the Foreign Minister of the Basque Government in Bilbao explaining that His Majesty's Government had approved the entry of 2,000 children into England. Arrangements had been agreed with the Basque representatives in London - the children would be drafted into institutions in groups of no fewer than fifty.

Leah Manning's response was characteristically swift and strongly worded. It was impossible to discriminate among the children already chosen. Since the Roman Catholics were willing to take 1,200 directly, the Salvation Army 500 and the camp at Southampton could hold 2,000, in Mrs Manning's opinion, it was worthwhile trying to persuade the Home Office to revise its numbers. In her first cable of that day, the *Habana* was still in port; by the time she sent her second, it was to report that the Basque Government had been obliged to send the ship with 4,000 civilians to Bordeaux and it would be returning on the Tuesday at the earliest. According to this cable, Stevenson was questioning whether the funds raised in England would be sufficient to support the children.

Not only Mrs Manning fired off salvoes at the luckless Roberts that day. Dr Audrey Russell, one of the doctors sent over to examine the children, also cabled on 15 May. In her view, it was too bad that boats for children were being diverted to evacuate moneyed people because HMG could not make up its mind quick enough. The question of available funds was being used as an excuse and, in this context, she urged Roberts to contact anyone influential with money, naming by way of example - Anstey, Garland, Clark, Sally, Melchett, Laughton. The boat would be available the following week and there was consternation at the thought of having to choose 2,000: the funds committed had to be doubled.

The following day cables went out from Philip Jordan, confirming that the *Habana* could handle 4,000 passengers and from Mrs Manning to the effect that Dr Ellis was flying home to place the facts before the Home Office and satisfy them that the Committee was competent to deal with 4,000.

The contradictions in the flow of cables winging their way between England and the Basque country are apparent. Clearly, if the Committee had at any stage intended to bring over 4,000, this was not communicated to the Home and Foreign Offices. Mrs Manning appears to have made promises to the Basque Government, which she was then very worried she would not be able to fulfil. The people in Bilbao were forcing the hand of those in London in order to ensure that the maximum number of children were allowed into England. Additionally, it seems that those in Bilbao, who were under tremendous pressure and running the risks of daily air raids while trying to make all the necessary preparations for the evacuation of the children, were not at all convinced that Roberts and the other members of the National Joint Committee in London were putting forward the case for 4,000 forcefully enough.

This could not be said of a cable sent by the Duchess of Atholl to Secretary of State Eden on 15 May:

'Mrs Leah Manning representing in Bilbao my committee for Spanish Relief cables terrible concern there because reception only 2000 children sanctioned STOP Basque Government had asked us to take 4000 She cables they specifically desire 4000 to include girls about 15 to save them from terrible fate if Moors enter STOP We have 18000 Pounds housing for some hundred over 2000 new houses offered daily and camp organised S'oton Saturday earliest refugees arrival STOP Very great public interest in this and fear wide spread feeling if 4000 refused under circumstances mentioned also fear much feeling Spain

STOP Am writing Simon can you help'

Two days later, Mrs Manning turned her attention to the proposal that 2,000 children might be put off at Bordeaux and the remaining 2,000 go on to England. Although the Asistencia Social had agreed to the children's going to Bordeaux, the French Consul had received no instructions. 4,000 could sail on Thursday (May 20) if all were sorted out at the London end. The pro-Consul cabled the Foreign Office to waive the age and sex-distribution limits that had been set. This cable, which made clear that it was sent at Mrs Manning's request, stated that to carry out the Foreign Office's full requirements would mean another 7-10 days delay. The balance of the sexes was very nearly equal and a proportion of older children was necessary to look after the younger members of families. Additionally, a major concern of the Home Office was answered: 'It is expected that all older children will go into catholic institutions so that no difficulties re. labour market will arise.'

On 18 May, Roberts received a telegram from the Duchess of Atholl, giving him instructions before a meeting at the Home Office. In particular, he was to re-emphasize the dangers to civilians, referring to a letter from Del Vayo to Eden in which he had told him of the rape of 12-year-old girls by Franco's Moorish soldiers. Roberts also heard from Mrs Manning, urging that the authorisation was needed within the next few hours for the 2000 children to disembark at Bordeaux or otherwise their places would be taken up by Government refugees on the *Habana*.

Following the meeting at the Home Office, Roberts sent three telegrams, the timing of which indicates how fast events were moving. The first one, immediately after the meeting, indicates the strong hope that a larger number of children and extension of the age limits would be granted while the French Consul should now have been given authority for the landing of 2,000 in France. At 3pm the second cable was sent, confirming that authorisation from Paris had been sent and that Ellis was returning to Bilbao. By 7pm, however, Roberts was able to cable triumphantly that a maximum of 4,000 children had been granted permission to come to England, the age limits now being set between five and fifteen and preference to be given to older girls. The French arrangements were cancelled and Roberts concluded by congratulating Mrs Manning.

The success of the National Joint Committee in obtaining this permission for the larger number of children to come to England should not be underrated, particularly given the attitudes of certain key officials and, also, the early views of Mr Golden, the Secretary to the Save the Children Fund in London.

E N Cooper, an official at the Home Office, transmitted on 5 May to W St C H Roberts at the Foreign Office the views Mr Golden had expressed during a telephone conversation the previous day. During this conversation, Cooper had learnt from Mr Golden of the preparations going on at Southampton, about which the Home Office then knew nothing. Golden then referred to the report in *The Times* that Leah Manning had proposed the removal of 4,000 children to the UK, for which purpose the President of the Basque Delegation in London had been authorised to charter a vessel. Golden was 'absolutely opposed in principle to the removal of young children from their native country' since such removal would cause them to deteriorate physically, morally and mentally.

He considered that the desire to evacuate the children was activated largely by political motives and could not understand why the committee (the National Joint Committee) did not consider a plan to remove the children to some other part of Spain. He was afraid that those people who were genuinely interested in the children were overwhelmed by those 'who wish to make political capital out of the imminent catastrophe at Bilbao'. There was the possibility that the children would be sent before permission were given and that the Foreign Office and Treasury would find themselves involved, against their will, in giving financial assistance to support the children - 'a consequence which some of its left-wing members such as Miss Ellen Wilkinson would no doubt welcome.'

Arising from Mr Golden's intervention, at least in part, the National Joint Committee was promptly informed that it was, under no circumstances, to bring children unless it could satisfy the Home Secretary's requirements. These were sent by telegram to Stevenson in Bilbao on 5 May - the number of children had to be in strict accord with the means at the Committee's disposal, the Committee should be prepared eventually to repatriate the children to Spain when conditions allowed, and there should be no charge on public funds for the children's maintenance.

Sir Henry Chilton's attitude towards foreign refugees, as expressed in a personal note from him to Mounsey, is illuminating:

'I don't blame the French if they are not enthusiastic about housing any more foreigners. The country is already overrun, with refugees from Russia and Germany and with Italians who don't relish Mussolini, while the Red Spaniards already here have given a lot of trouble, especially at Lyons.'

Sir Geoffrey Mounsey was even less enthusiastic towards the evacuation than Chilton and, indeed, favoured a proposal by Franco that a neutral zone be set up in Spain for refugees. On 11 May, he wrote, 'If it is desired to pursue General Franco's practical suggestion and free our navy from their increasingly embarrassing protective duties', the suggestion could be put forward to the Basque Government. HMG might discontinue and ask the Basques and French to stop evacuations 'as soon as it is clear that the land scheme is acceptable to all parties'. Not surprisingly, the scheme did not meet with favour from the Republican side; Azcarate informed the Foreign Office that the Spanish Government considered that if they agreed to a neutral zone, this would imply the acceptance of unrestricted bombing of the evacuated areas. Mounsey minuted on 20 May, 'It seems useless to pursue the matter with such unhelpful and uncompromising combatants.'

Chapter Five

Arrival in England

'Basque Children greet England with a Cheer'

(*Southern Daily Echo*, May 24, 1937)

With the go-ahead from London, preparations for the evacuation proceeded with speed. Trainloads of children, 600 at a time, rolled up to San Turce and were put on board the *Habana* throughout Thursday 20 May. Before the children could go on board, however, there was fairly intensive bombing of the port area - some forty-five bombs were dropped in the vicinity according to the captain of the liner, Ricardo Fernandez, although he stated at the time that the bombers' target was uncertain.

The liner had been built originally for 1,500 passengers, so the children and accompanying adults were very cramped and had to settle into any corner of available space they could find. The President of the Basque Government, Aguirre, came on board to bid goodbye to the 'brave expeditionary infants', as the children were called in the local press, and then the ship was able to set sail early on the morning of the 21st. Outside the three-mile limit, the battleship *Royal Oak* and two destroyers, *Fearless* and *Foxhound*, formed a convoy for the *Habana* and the yacht *Goizeko-Izarra*, which was taking other evacuees to France. *Fearless* accompanied the *Habana* all the way to the Needles while *Foxhound* escorted the yacht to Bordeaux.

The *Habana* was left alone by Insurgent ships; doubtless the British convoy was a significant factor but so too were the sea conditions which were terrible throughout the Bay of Biscay. One of the teachers who accompanied the children remembers that one of the priests was so violently seasick that, leaning over the rails, he lost his dentures into the raging firmament below. Only a week after the journey, Dr Ellis published a very brief account of the journey in *The New Statesman and Nation* in which he graphically described the conditions on board and the atmosphere among the children:

'Four thousand wretchedly seasick children crowded into an old boat whose very latrines are apt to regurgitate in sympathy, are not a pretty sight. Fortunately, by evening they were all falling asleep from sheer exhaustion where they lay. Under the direction of the captain himself (who had filled his own cabin with children), the stewards cleaned the saloons where most of the children were sleeping, and spread sheets over the palliases. We collected sleeping children from all over the ship, picking them off ladders, window sills, and out of baths and laying them under cover. Next morning I was awakened by the sound of thousands of feet on deck, and going out was greeted with cries of 'Rubio!' 'Hombre!' and asked perhaps five hundred times when we should arrive, and whether they would really get white bread, and butter - and milk - and even meat, in England.'

The ship dropped anchor in Southampton Water in the early evening of 22 May, when a barge went out to meet the ship. On board were Dr Williams, the Medical Officer of Health of Southampton, Henry Brinton, a member of the National Joint Committee, customs and immigration officials, and food and sweets for the children. There were very few bystanders as the people of Southampton had been asked not to come in crowds to watch since, as recorded by the *Southern Daily Echo*, the state of health of the children was unknown. There were, however, a few representatives of the Salvation Army on the quayside and this greatly puzzled some of the children who had not realised that the English dressed up in uniform.

Fig 3. Children on board the Habana. (From a fund-raising leaflet issued by the National Joint Committee.)

One of the first visitors on board in the morning was Sra Azcarate, the wife of the Spanish Ambassador, and the Basque priests who had travelled with the children celebrated a Mass at the stern end of the ship, for those who wished to attend. One child, Felix Gonzalez, was taken off early to go to hospital for a minor operation. Despite the Home Office's age limits, at least one very young passenger came on the Habana - a two-months-old baby accompanied by his very own private nurse and shown in press photographs happily smiling to his fellow evacuees after the rigours of the bumpy journey.

The Health Authorities required a medical inspection before the children could go to the camp and at the end of this each child was issued with a coloured band - white for clean and blue for infectious or contagious. Red bands were issued to those who had to be taken to the public baths for disinfestation, to have their clothes replaced with new ones and their hair cropped very short. These actions immediately marked out these children from the rest and at first they were very self-conscious of their short hair and apparent branding as dirty. In reality, many of these children had been sleeping rough in appalling conditions for some time before their arrival and the number requiring this treatment (under 20 per cent of the total) was reassuringly low.

Waves of green double decker buses, on free loan from the Hants & Dorset company, transported the children to the camp at Stoneham, where a frenzy of activity greeted them among the 500 bell tents erected on the buttercup-covered fields, which have disappeared nowadays to make way for a hypermarket. Not surprisingly, since the camp was originally established for only 2,000 children, volunteers, including the Duchess of Atholl, were still making last-minute preparations when the children arrived. Of the nearly 4,000 children on board the liner, some 3,000 disembarked on the Sunday and the remainder the next day - a disembarkation rate which was gratifyingly speedy in the eyes of the organisers.

Fig 4. Basque children enjoying a first meal at Stoneham Camp (Daily Herald, 24 May 1937)

At the camp, the first meal the children had on English soil comprised soup, white bread, fruit and a cup of milk. A number of visitors came to the camp including Sir John and Lady Simon and Lord Rhayeder who was quoted in *The Yorkshire Post* as describing the camp as, 'the most touching thing I have known in all my political life.' Motorists passing by also stopped to see what was going on and handed out sweets and cigarettes (a large number of the boys smoked).

The noise and probable lack of organisation can only be guessed at but there were undoubtedly significant problems of communication and understanding. Few of the volunteers spoke Spanish, the children spoke either Spanish or Basque or both but very little English. They had never been camping before and were certainly not particularly disciplined as a whole. They had travelled over a rough sea to a strange land and were not at all sure when next they would see the rest of their families or their country (though it has to be said that most had been told they would be going to England for at most a few months).

The camp organisers were probably more than a little relieved when the long, dry spell that England had been enjoying that early summer gave way to a tremendous rainstorm the first night the children arrived, forcing them under canvas as early as 7.30pm.

The British press reported the arrival of the children in sympathetic terms with headlines such as 'Basque Babies in Britain' and 'Basque Children Greet England with a Cheer'. The *Southern Daily Echo*, Southampton's local paper, carried a full-page article that included greetings to the children in Spanish and 'a children's patriotic song' of Spain. The article finished with a plea for help from any drivers willing to ferry volunteers to and from the camp. Indeed, local support would appear to have been quite strong at the beginning - the day before the *Habana*'s arrival, the Mayor of Southampton chaired a meeting at which £157 was collected for the cause. But it soon became clear that not all officialdom nor public opinion was favourably disposed towards the arrival of the children.

On 20 May, the Town Clerk to the Borough of Eastleigh, which contained Stoneham, wrote to the National Joint Committee to 'get certain points settled'. The annoyance felt by the Eastleigh Town Council at not being consulted on the choice of the site for the camp is apparent from the following:

'Your Committee has seen fit to choose a site for dumping almost unpreparedly some 4,000 young foreign children, without the foresight and the courtesy of letting us know anything whatsoever about it - our only information is that of press and handbill, rumour and enquiry. It has done so with as little regard to local conditions as to local costs, and after discussion with colleagues within and without the Borough I am bound to write...'

Two major concerns were worrying Eastleigh at the time - whether the borough would be liable for any medical charges incurred through the treatment of any children under the aegis of the Southampton Medical Officer of Health, who had offered to accept patients from the camp in a new section of his smallpox wards, and the fact that they considered the camp to have been poorly conceived and laid out in the first place. Wilfrid Roberts's reply shows that the Committee had thought they fell under Southampton's jurisdiction and not Eastleigh's; and that the National Joint Committee fully accepted liability for any medical costs. On the other point, however, Roberts expressed surprise since the organiser of the camp, Mr Sams, 'is very experienced in organising refugee camps' and they had, moreover, benefited from military advice as well as from the Ministry of Health and Dame Janet Campbell. Future events were to show that the Eastleigh officials were rather more correct in their estimation of the camp's set-up.

Medical concerns were a regular feature of certain people's reactions to the influx of the Basque children. Although they had been examined in Bilbao and found, in general, to be in very good condition by Drs Ellis and Russell and had been examined once more on disembarkation, on 26 May yet another medical examination took place, this time at the camp. On 25 May, Lord Lloyd in the House of Lords had warned against the dangers of the children bringing with them trachoma, a contagious form of conjunctivitis, and, although such apprehensions were unfounded, an ophthalmologist was brought into the camp to allay any fears. The question of trachoma had, in fact, already been raised as early as 15 May at a meeting at the Home Office, when Dame Janet Campbell stated that the two doctors carrying out medical examinations in Bilbao 'were taking every care to select healthy children with particular reference to trachoma, which is stated to be a fairly common complaint in the Basque Country.'

Parliamentary Questions in the House of Commons in the

following weeks also seemed to dwell at great length on the health of the children. On 7 June, Miss Cazalet asked what the general position was regarding the health of the children. The Minister of Health confirmed the general good health of the children but also emphasised the need to evacuate the camp as quickly as possible. He added that there had been five cases of typhoid, two cases of diphtheria and three cases of measles and the patients had been isolated and appropriate precautionary measures taken. Captain Harold Balfour, clearly not a champion of the cause, was not impressed and claimed evidence that there were no adequate medical arrangements, half-time voluntary helpers for approximately 100 patients (in reality, at that time there were thirty-one patients in Isolation, thirty-four children at Moor Hill and eight children in hospital at Southampton) and tremendous language problems. Other MPs tried to make the Minister of Health accept some responsibility for the health of the children but all he would reply was that a medical officer of the Ministry regularly visited the camp and reported back.

On 8 June the House was diverted by the question of the cost of Government tents at the camp but Thursday 10 June saw MPs back again at the subject closest to their hearts, the threat to the health of British citizens from the Basque children. Questions were asked about the inoculation and vaccination of the children and the number of cases of typhoid or suspected cases that had arisen. Certain MPs made their fears quite clear, 'In view of the risk of the spread of this disease, would the right honourable Gentleman give an assurance that none of the children will be allowed to move to other parts of the country until they have undergone full quarantine?' (Sir A Southby)

'Does the right honourable Gentleman realise that some of these children have already been removed from the camp and that some of them are in my constituency? Have the necessary steps been taken between the Ministry of Health and the local authorities to make sure that the children are fit to be removed?' (Sir J Haslam)

The tone of self-righteous concern can be clearly detected in these questions and although the Minister answered in measured and careful terms, making clear that he was happy that matters were being dealt with appropriately, perhaps the better response was that of Mr Davidson who suggested, 'Would the Minister arrange for a supply of tabloids to honourable members opposite who are afraid of infection?'

The visits by medical officers to the camp were frequent, as stated by Mr Bernays in his reply of 7 June. The reports made by one of the officers, Dr W S Craig, were very detailed but even-handed in their approach. Dr Craig genuinely appreciated the great difficulties under which the Camp's administration was labouring and appears to have tried to put forward recommendations that were essentially practicable. Copies of these reports were forwarded, via the Home Office, to Wilfrid Roberts.

Craig's second interim report, dated 25 May (an indication of the importance attached to questions of health) makes for interesting reading and throws a number of insights on to the conditions in the camp. Almost inevitably, Dr Craig did not confine himself to medical problems but began with some general remarks on the administration of the camp. Perhaps not surprisingly, voluntary workers tended 'to select duties according to their own tastes', not helped by the fact that duties were rather vaguely defined throughout the camp. Dr Craig was critical of the rather limited help being given by the adult refugees, the auxiliares and teachers, and also noted that 'some resentment was heard expressed by voluntary workers at the apparent inactivity of priests'. He also passed subtle sentence on the translators- 'there is need for additional competent interpreters' (Craig's underlining).

In addition, Dr Craig made four major recommendations:

1. Speedy evacuation of the camp
2. Efficient control of the camp boundaries (regardless of cost)
3. Constant, effective supervision of adolescents
4. The provision of an independent, effectively barriered isolation unit within the camp

The greatest concern was undoubtedly the danger of any infection spreading through the camp. Both Dr Craig and Dr Taylor, the Medical Superintendent of the camp, believed that the speedy clearance of the camp was paramount. An indication of the concern felt by the medics was Dr Taylor's intention to have each child medically examined each alternate day. Dr Craig agreed that given the size of the medical staff (four other full-time doctors and one part-time local GP) that 'any attempt to conduct a more frequent inspection would defeat its own purpose by being too summary.' It is unclear how the doctors were in any event going to meet their already ambitious target.

Secure camp boundaries were necessary both for the safety of the children and also to prevent their breaking out of camp and getting into mischief, which had clearly already been the case although the camp had been operational for barely two days. One suggestion from Dr Craig was to erect a canvas screen on the road side of the camp - 'the value of such a screen would be many times that of the estimated cost of £35.'

Although not going into details, the meaning of Dr Craig's comments on the problems of the adolescent children is quite clear. The need for closer supervision was underscored by the remarks made on the state of Moorhill House, a building close by which was being used to house non-acute medical cases. The VADs on night duty at Moorhill had found it impossible 'to keep children in their bed and to prevent older children of different sexes mixing.'

The need for an isolation unit within the camp was obvious - to isolate possibly infectious children without over-taxing the more formal medical facilities.

It is difficult to gauge how effective the camp administration was in carrying out Dr Craig's recommendations on such matters as supervision of the older children and boundaries, but it is clear that a fairly complex system of camp patrols was instituted and that a double fence was erected on the perimeter of the camp. The isolation unit was set up though it was several weeks before Dr Craig was totally satisfied with it. Visits by Dr Craig were exceptionally frequent in the first few weeks of the camp's life but then tailed off naturally as the number of children in the camp reduced through dispersal to the colonies being set up elsewhere in the country.

Chapter Six

The Camp at Stoneham

'Rather than say it was a dirty Camp, I would say it was an untidy Camp.'

(Duchess of Atholl to Wilfrid Roberts)

Running a camp for 4,000 children would have been a huge undertaking if the children had spoken English and had had some understanding of the requirements of the camping life. Given that the children spoke Spanish or Basque and that this was their first experience of a camp under canvas, the undertaking was almost foolhardy in the difficulties it created. Problems were inevitable, particularly given the very little time available to set up the camp before the children arrived.

Although the camp was intended to last three to four weeks only, it was open from May until mid-September. During its nearly four months' existence it suffered from numerous changes of personnel, often due to ill-health which seems to have dogged the administration of the camp, and from an almost continuous fight against the dangers of disease, which in such an environment just might have led to an epidemic.

A picture of life at Stoneham was drawn up at the time for public consumption in a booklet written by Yvonne Cloud and called *The Basque Children in England.* Proceeds from the sales of this book went to the Basque Children's Committee and, naturally enough, the booklet concentrated on the happiness of the children at being safe among people who wanted to help them, and on anecdotes, such as the entertainments' officer's referring to the camp cinema as a case of 'putting all my Basques in one Exit', or the reaction of the children to the news that Bilbao had fallen to the insurgents.

A more accurate picture of life at the camp and also of the problems facing the administration is painted by the reports on the camp which were sent every few days by the chief administrator (Commandant of the Camp - a title unlikely to have found favour a few years later) to the Basque Children's Committee in the person of Wilfrid Roberts. These reports were official documents for circulation to other members of the Committee. Correspondence concerning Stoneham Camp with, primarily, the Organising Secretaries of the two Committees and Wilfrid Roberts but also from others adds further useful background information and insights into the conditions at Stoneham.

Unfortunately, Mr Sams, who set up the camp and was reputedly experienced with refugees, fell ill and resigned very early from his duties so that Henry Brinton, who had been acting as Sams's assistant, took over his duties on 24 May. The various organisations working at the camp - the British Red Cross, Boy Scouts and Girl Guides - became increasingly critical of the manner in which Brinton ran the camp: so much so that by the beginning of June they had given notice of withdrawing their assistance. The local Member of Parliament lodged a formal request that the camp be placed under the supervision of someone with more experience of camp life and the Ministry of Health made similar representations. At a meeting of the Basque Children's Committee on 7 July, Captain MacNamara suggested that a certain Major Irwin, just recently retired from the army, take over the running of the camp. The major was interviewed then and there and appointed at the salary of £1 per day, all found, to take up the post as soon as he could.

The Committee was anxious not to blame Henry Brinton for the problems that had arisen and, indeed, was very keen that he should remain and work with Major Irwin. Unfortunately, we do not have the letters which set out exactly how the Major was expected to run the camp and in what capacity Brinton was to continue to work but we do know from Major Irwin's covering letter to his first Camp Report that he was not totally happy about it, ' with such a system I cannot hold myself responsible for any action or policy which might be adopted........without my cognizance.'

The Duchess of Atholl put forward certain organisational recommendations in a private report sent to Roberts under cover of a note dated June 9 but evidently written some days earlier. These recommendations were clearly aimed at saving Brinton's face by redesignating his position (from Commandant to General Staff Officer) and changing the authority levels within the camp. Although pre-empted by the decision to appoint Major Irwin, the Duchess's report did highlight some of the key areas of concern within the camp.

The main problem areas of the camp, as the Duchess saw them, were sanitation, job definitions among the voluntary workers and general oversight of the children. The Duchess had some suitably wry comments for those on the outside who criticized the camp, 'a certain outside medical expert, and the writer of a certain adverse report criticised the latrines and urinals, and apparently wanted them made suitable for Life Guards, instead of tiny children.'

As to those areas where she could see there was room for improvement, she expressed herself with appropriate tact, 'rather than say it was a dirty Camp, I would say it was an untidy Camp.' 'Speaking generally of the personnel, it all seemed to me to be very keen and anxious to help... but there was a good deal of overlapping and changing of duties... In other words there seemed to be the cry 'Give me my job and I'll do it.' The Duchess continued, 'one of the principal troubles seems to me to be that you cannot leave the children alone for portions of the day, when you have done your work, in the way that you can leave soldiers. This means a larger staff and someone always on watch.'

Significantly. the Duchess suggested that an officer should be specifically in charge of the older boys, who had already proved to be extremely difficult to control and some of whom would provide the Basque Children's Committee with a real dilemma over the question of repatriation in the not too distant future.

Even more important were the Duchess's final comments at the end of her report concerning the attitude to be taken inside the camp towards events in Spain, 'One thing should be absolutely taboo in camp, and that is the discussion of politics, and as little sides as possible should be taken, in camp at least, with regard to the internal situation in Spain. Everyone is there to help helpless children, and no other question arises.' Evidently, other questions had arisen and the Duchess recognised the importance of maintaining an impartial stance, at least publicly, as far as Spain and the plight of the children were concerned.

From 11 June to 9 September, reports were regularly sent from the camp - twice a week until the last few weeks of the camp's life. Much of Major Irwin's time at the beginning was taken up with sorting out the sanitation arrangements and with improving the general discipline within the camp. He quickly appointed one NCO and six men to patrol the camp at night and almost immediately he increased the sanitation squad from twelve to eighteen since, in his opinion, the general standard of cleanliness was deplorable.

Irwin was keen to reduce the running costs of the camp as far as possible and, to this end, he reorganised the messing arrangements for the staff and children and sought to weed out hangers-on at the camp who came basically for the free meals but did very little work at the camp to justify their maintenance. That Major Irwin may not have been totally successful is reflected in a comment by his successor at the camp, Major Hunter, in a letter dated 11 August that they had to 'get rid of the parasites battening on the Committee'.

The costs of running the camp were significant. Accounts for the period from 23 May to 18 September show that a total of £18,992 had been spent in running the camp with an average weekly expenditure of around £1,117. The highest items of expenditure were food, which took up nearly half the budget, and then wages and health insurance. Other heavy items of expenditure were transport and medical costs.

The average weekly cost of maintaining a child was estimated at 15s 9d which was exceptionally close to the estimate of 15 shillings per week that Mr Golden of the Save the Children Fund had told the Home Office would be needed to maintain the children. Of the 15s 9d, 6s 7d went on food.

An enormous volume of camping equipment was required by the camp. Although Major Irwin could not send equipment back at as fast a rate as he would have liked, because of the slowing down in the evacuation of children from the camp, he was able to report that, by 9 July, one hundred bell tents had been returned, four hundred trestle tables, two hundred and sixty-eight forms and over six hundred and fifty blankets, as well as various types of portable stove and other kinds of tents and poles. Much of the equipment had been rented from Milletts and Sons, a company which appears to have become increasingly impatient with the camp over time and very critical of the condition in which equipment was returned. By August, Milletts was charging £50 per week on unreturned goods as compensation for damages. In spite of this, Major Hunter, then in charge of the camp, still hoped to negotiate a discount, to be set off against the then current account and any future charges, given the large overall size of the business. It is doubtful that he succeeded.

The first complete census of the children in camp was taken in mid-June. This found that 2,715 children were in the lines, 32 in Isolation, 35 at Moorhill, 19 in local hospitals and 1,025 already sent elsewhere. This came to a total of 3,826 children as having been evacuated from Bilbao. There seems initially to have been some confusion about how many children were evacuated - at the first meeting of the Basque Children's Committee, Captain MacNamara told the Committee that 3,840 children had disembarked; in answer to a Parliamentary Question, a Minister replied that 3,881 children arrived at North Stoneham; Stevenson cabled from Bilbao that 3,900 children had been evacuated.

This state of confusion persisted for some time. In September, fifteen children whose names were on a duplicate list held in the Basque country could not be traced from the lists at Stoneham. After some checking, it was found that thirteen of the fifteen never embarked. Of the remaining two, Major Hunter reported 'one of them would appear to be a small boy who has been in camp from the beginning and has never been able to give either his name or number.'. The other one, Manuel Vilares Fernandez, No. 3527, had disembarked at Southampton but had not been traced.

According to a report by Lilian Smith, made in early September, keeping track of the children was not made any easier by the laxness of camp discipline, which seems to have deteriorated with the departure of the stern Major Irwin. 'There is no proper central control on the movements of the children - they wander into the villages and elsewhere without escorts and return when they like, many of them missing meals, and it was admitted that some of them slept out of camp.' Under such circumstances, it was, not surprisingly, difficult to arrive at an accurate estimate of the number of children left in the camp.

Miss Smith had gone to Stoneham precisely to obtain the exact name and number of every child who had by then not yet been evacuated. She was frustrated in this but was able to deduce the number of children who should still have been in the camp in a somewhat roundabout way:

No of children in Bible	4159
No of duplicate numbers	7
	4152
Embarkation number	3827
No of cancellations should be	325
No in Bible not indexed	626
Less no of cancellations	325
No in Camp should be	301

The 'Bible' was the master list assembled in Bilbao by Mrs Manning and the cancellations would have been those children on the list who never made it to the *Habana* for one reason or another.

A large staff of volunteers and paid workers was employed by the camp. A list compiled in July shows there were more than 80 paid part- and full-time staff. The highest paid were the doctors at seven guineas per week and the Matron at three guineas. The standard wage for most jobs was £2.10s although the women employed in various capacities in the camp were paid consistently below this sum - interpreters receiving £1.10s per week and the women assisting in the children's mess tents only £1, or less than half the pay of the waiters in the staff mess. It is not difficult to guess which of these two jobs was the more demanding. (Taking inflation into account, £1 in 1937 roughly equates to £73 today. So, a weekly salary of seven guineas would, in today's money, be the equivalent of about £537 per week.)

With such a large staff, occasionally someone turned out to be less than trustworthy but Major Irwin dealt swiftly with any such abuses. In his seventh Camp Report he notes that a court case took place on the preceding Monday concerning some petty stealing at the camp. He felt sure this would prove a salutary lesson to any in the camp who had intentions themselves to steal and would also show the outside world that the camp administration would not tolerate abuse of the position of trust in which they found themselves. At around the same time, Irwin had to sack the Supply Officer (for reasons unspecified) but was pleased to be able to replace him with an ex-QM from the King's Dragoon Guards.

While most of the major's reports are taken up with the big questions of ensuring adequate sanitation in the camp, bringing down costs and endeavouring to maintain discipline, he also found the time to consider problems such as the education outlook for at least some of the children. He also anticipated the need to keep the children as occupied as possible during the day. One of the criticisms levelled against the Committees that organised the evacuation of the children has been that they all but neglected the educational needs of their charges - Major Irwin, however, took the time to emphasize in one of his reports the view of the Senior Medical Officer 'that some of the older boys in camp are of University standard. I consider that the committee might consider the proposal of allowing these youths to continue their education.'

He also anticipated that there would be problems should Bilbao fall and that some means of entertaining the children needed to be found 'to keep (them) from brooding'. As it was, when the fall of Bilbao was announced to the children, after the initial reactions of grief and, in some cases, of children running away from camp, Major Irwin was quite clear what the best solution would be: to clear the camp as quickly as possible.

Interesting light is shed on the relations between the organisers and the Roman Catholic church by Major Irwin's description of and conclusions from a conversation he had with Father Hurley, the Church's representative at the camp. The latter complained that the priests were not allowed sufficient supervision over the evacuations to non-Catholic homes to which Major Irwin 'pointed out that evacuations to homes could not be held up or numbers not completed pending the settlement of the dispute as regards whether a child had been baptised or not.' Irwin believed that the religious question might be used to ensure that a maximum number of children would be accepted into Catholic homes.

Why this should have been a problem is not clear since, after all, one of the main selling points for bringing the children over had been that they would be going to Catholic institutions; on the other hand, it is also certain that a number of the people involved in looking after the children regarded the Church with some suspicion as being pro-Franco and liable to repatriate children as quickly as possible.

The removal of children from the camp to homes scattered throughout the country was fast-moving during June and then became slower and slower through July, August and September. Although partially impeded by the need to put the camp into quarantine from time to time and, in July, to inoculate the children against typhoid, there were other reasons for a slow-down in the rate of evacuation such as the fact that in the first month it was the large institutions such as the Salvation Army and the Roman Catholic church which were taking away significant numbers of children at a time; as the summer wore on, it was the turn of local voluntary groups to raise the money and find the accommodation for children.

Some bad publicity arising from the antics of a few of the older boys did not help in efforts to raise funds. Tellingly, the Roman Catholic institutions ran out of Catholics from the camp by mid-July as they only had room left for girls. It was recognised that the real difficulty now lay in placing the older boys. A census taken on July 22 underscored the point; of the children left in camp or under medical supervision, 476 were boys compared with only 197 girls.

Major Irwin saw the camp through its first two months but had to leave his post 'for personal reasons' in early July. A temporary replacement for two weeks then gave way to Major Neil Hunter who ran the camp until it finally disbanded, although his stay was far beyond what he had originally intended. While Hunter's task may have been slightly easier than that facing Irwin, he still had to contend with some very serious problems notably the maintenance of cleanliness and discipline, neither of which proved easy.

An early move was to make a section of the field near the road out of bounds. This was just after a little girl had been involved in a serious accident on that stretch of road. The other reason Hunter gave for cordoning off this parcel of ground was to avoid the danger of any 'undesirable contacts', which might be regretted later.

Hunter also had the unhappy task of dealing with the first death in the camp, that of a maestra, Encarnacion de Belasco, who died in the camp hospital of chronic heart disease. She was buried according to the Catholic rite at Eastleigh Cemetery but provision was made for her body to be exhumed for re-burial in Spain should this be desired at some later stage by her family. Aside from the death and the car accident, there was also an unfortunate increase in the number of children who were becoming verminous. Eventually Hunter took the decision to move the remaining 'Spanish lines' and change the bedding (after twelve weeks). He proved right in his decision insofar as the incidence of scabies reduced significantly thereafter. By this time, the children, who had been benefiting from the existence of twenty-four showers, instead of the original twelve intended to cope with the bathing needs of these thousands of children, now had hot baths available as well.

As if the real problems were not bad enough, Major Hunter also had to deal with some imaginary ones. In a letter to Wilfrid Roberts dated August 17, he relates how Miss Arne had telephoned him about rumours that 'most of these Basque women have become pregnant' while when Nancy Adams (of the TUC) had been visiting the camp she had spoken of a rumour that prostitutes had smuggled themselves on board the *Habana* and that this 'outrageous story has now reached local yachting circles'. To stop such unpleasant stories gaining any further ground, Hunter enclosed a copy of a note from Dr Daly, then in charge of the camp's medical services, to the effect that two of the Spanish women were pregnant but were married and had been pregnant before they left Spain. Dr Daly knew of no other cases of pregnancy within the camp.

With fewer children in camp, preparations had to be made for the winding down of activities at Stoneham altogether. Staffing was run down and non-essential services curtailed. In late August the camp hospital was closed and various outside contractors' services terminated, including a firm with the engaging name of Switchit Services Ltd, which had provided the camp radio system and electrical lighting in the most important administrative offices. Key staff were leaving as well, notably Mr Ainsworth who had been in charge of evacuations of the children to their new homes and had been responsible, in Major Hunter's words, for 'well over 400,000 child miles'.

The smaller numbers also made excursions or group activities easier to organise. Quite early in August, the children went on a day trip to Bournemouth, enjoying a picnic lunch in the New Forest followed by a swim, courtesy of the City Corporation, and free seats at the local cinema. In September, a Sports Day was arranged for the fifteenth with prizes to be given out by the Mayor of Eastleigh. The Sports Day was open to the public and Hunter was able to report on the twelfth that the children were practising hard for their individual events. The reason given by Major Hunter for putting on the Sports Day was 'with a view to keeping the children as much as possible in Camp during the last week.' The reasoning is perhaps indicative of the difficulties being encountered in trying to keep the remaining children under control (as Lilian Smith had mentioned in her brief report).

In August, Wilfrid Roberts expressed the wish to have both Hunter and Ainsworth at the Basque Children's Committee's headquarters, once the camp was closed, to deal with the tricky and increasingly sensitive issue of repatriation. Betty Arne pointed out to Roberts that he should avoid announcing Hunter's appointment just yet since 'part of the problem in trying to house children stems from people's conviction that children will shortly be repatriated'. The charitable impulses of people clearly required that they have the children for a satisfyingly lengthy period of time; even though it had been publicly stated that the children should be repatriated as soon as this were practicable, volunteers were unwilling to recognise this as a possibility in the near future.

From September, some concern began to be expressed about the inadequacy of the children's clothing to withstand the rigours of an English winter. Even without the requirement for additional heavier clothing, much of the children's existing clothing was looking very threadbare and had to be replaced. The question of winter clothing was, however, put off for as long as possible in the hope that the children would all be evacuated to homes which would then take on responsibility for their clothing.

The 22nd and last report from Stoneham was dated September 12. The camp was closed on September 18 when there were only some 200 children and about 35 Spanish adults, including three priests. The children and staff remaining with them moved to what became known as the Basque Children's Evacuation Centre at New Romney in Kent. That such a high proportion of Spanish adults were still at Stoneham is not too surprising when we note what Lilian Smith had to say about the female helpers who had been brought over:

'The Senoritas present a far more difficult problem than the actual children. Most of them are entirely out of hand and go in and out of the camp as they please and are allowed to refuse to go to centres if they don't want to go. They are also (with a few exceptions) most negligent concerning their charges.'

From the beginnings of the camp, the administrators were disappointed with the attitude of the young women who had been brought over to help look after the children. In many ways, it would seem that the older girls among the children were far more responsible towards the little ones; too many of the señoritas enjoyed having a good time rather than fulfilling their responsibilities.

Of the staff who had come and gone at Stoneham Camp, at least one, Neville Towne, appears to have been dismissed in part because of his political views. Towne was appointed the Entertainments Officer and after an initial period of illness appears to have been quite successful in organising entertainment for the children, at least in the eyes of Major Irwin, particularly after he gained the assistance of four university students.

Early in July, Major Irwin recommended that Towne should go to the Deal camp for boys, stating that he had 'the necessary personality to control the boys, provided he is given an adequate staff'. By August, however, the opinion in the head office of the Basque Children's Committee had been influenced by others more critical of Towne's performance.

In particular, on 26 July Ernest Brown, a member of the National Joint Committee and also of the Relief Committee for Victims of Fascism, wrote to Wilfrid Roberts to complain about the continued employment of Towne. He argued strongly that, during his time at Stoneham, Towne had accomplished very little, having organised no daily programme of entertainments or sport to keep the children happily occupied - only accepting and arranging a few musical recitals and a concert party or two, which held very little interest for the children. Brown added that Dr Audrey Russell fully agreed with his analysis. The second reason for Brown's disquiet at the employment of Towne was his attitude towards the children. He had been heard to advise visitors to the camp not to offer sweets to the children but rather to give them to English children because, 'they would have appreciated them better than these brats', and he was reported as having referred to the children as swine. The cheers at Towne's departure from the camp were, in Brown's view, cheers that he was leaving and not cheers of appreciation for his work.

In mid-August, Betty Arne wrote that very little result had been seen for the £29 3s 8d that Towne had cost thus far, that he had visited homes giving the impression he was on some kind of official inspection, although his only concern was Entertainments, and he had talked at length not to the local organisers but to the children. Some children had complained that he was a fascist and he had made certain 'indiscreet' remarks at the Worthing home.

Requested by Roberts to give a full report on his activities in visiting the homes, Towne drew up a lengthy letter on August 30 in which he defended his record strongly, stating that he had achieved a number of positive improvements at various homes such as free or reduced charge entry to local cinemas and similar concessions at amusement parks or seaside attractions. He had also been involved in setting up sporting arrangements - including contacting the Secretaries of numerous football clubs including Brighton and Hove Albion, Exeter City, Bristol City, Bristol Rovers, West Bromwich Albion, Everton and Preston North End, all of which had promised to send old footballs and kit to various homes. The same was true of some rugby clubs - Newport, Plymouth Albion and Birkenhead Park. Some of the clubs had also agreed to arrange some football matches with their juniors.

Towne declared that he always visited the homes (38 in all) in his capacity as Entertainments Officer but that at some of the homes he had been invited to look around and had been asked to assist in minor difficulties which had arisen. He had been asked to write articles for the local press and to speak at local theatres and functions and this he had done readily. He claimed to have received many letters of thanks from Secretaries of the local committees, and pointed out that to visit such a large number of homes 'without unconsciously offending someone' was not easy. He finished his letter by declaring how much he cared for the children and how much he would like to continue with his present work or be allowed to assist in any other way.

Towne's arguments did not cut much ice and he was dismissed. He wrote to Wilfrid Roberts on September 1, expressing regret at being relieved of his duties and asking for some form of financial assistance so that he could repair the damage sustained by some of his clothing during the course of his duties.

Roberts replied in an understanding and conciliatory manner and undertook to see what he could do for the unfortunate Towne. The same day that Roberts replied to Towne, the Basque Children's Committee office received a request for information about Towne from the Grange Home for Spanish Refugee Children in Street, one of the local homes for the Basque children, to which Towne had applied for voluntary work. Wilfrid Roberts replied promptly giving a very guarded view about the desirability of employing Towne:

'I think it ought to be possible to make use of Mr Towne in the way you suggest. He speaks fluent Spanish but I must warn you that he is a contentious character. There are some people who think his work at the Camp was valuable and he did organise a great many entertainments for the children, and he is undoubtedly popular amongst many of the children. On the other hand, there are both children and workers who have been critical of him. His sympathies are on the side of the insurgents and we have had complaints as to his tact. However, with the shortage of competent Spanish speaking people, I think it should be possible to make use of Mr Towne, laying down clearly there must be no political discussion and insisting on regular routine.'

Not surprisingly, Towne was not offered a post at Street.

Shortly afterwards, Towne wrote again to Wilfrid Roberts, this time with the news that he had received a cable from Argentina telling him of his father's death. Since his allowance would automatically stop until his father's affairs were sorted out, he asked if Roberts couldn't find some way of placing him somewhere until matters were sorted out.

Roberts sent him a brief note on 16 September in which he undertook to see what could be done when he went up to London the following weekend. This was in spite of the action taken by Miss McDiarmid, the Assistant Organising Secretary of the Basque Children's Committee, which she recorded on the same day that Roberts wrote to Towne. Her action arose from reports that Towne had visited the Worthing centre, staying overnight and stating that he was going to arrange some football matches for the boys. He left the next morning, having done nothing but the Assistant Secretary had also heard that he had applied for the post of Warden at Brighton. She immediately sent out a notice to all centres, stating that Towne was no longer associated with the organisation and that he should not be allowed access to the homes.

No more is heard of the unhappy Mr Towne. Roberts's attitude appears somewhat ambivalent in the affair, as though he did not wish to hurt Towne' s feelings. The Secretaries in the head office, however, appear to have been in no doubt at all about the unsuitability of Neville Towne. It is clear that his presumed sympathies with the insurgents weighed very heavily against him. Further, while his letters to Roberts almost rival Uriah Heep in their tone of unctuous humility, he does not appear to have wasted any time in trying to obtain positions for himself in various homes, possibly not realising that the homes would automatically refer back to the head office.

Chapter Seven

Committees and Yet More Committees

'Mrs Miller reported on the constitutional position between the two Committees, which was not at all clear. It was recognised that there was no difference in policy between the two Committees.'

(Minutes of the National Joint Committee, 11 October 1937)

The force behind the evacuation of the children was the National Joint Committee for Spanish Relief. Very quickly, however, a new, less overtly political, committee was set up to deal exclusively with the Basque Children, the Basque Children's Committee.

The people sitting on both committees came by and large from the relatively affluent upper and middle classes of British society. Several were MPs or professionals in medicine, journalism or academia. A significant number appear to have been wealthy young ladies prone to good works. Additionally, there were the religious representatives and trade unionists.

Of the MPs on these two main committees, two were Unionist (Conservative), Captain JRJ MacNamara and the Duchess of Atholl; the others were Wilfrid Roberts (Liberal) and, for Labour, Ellen Wilkinson, David Grenfell, Philip Noel-Baker and Eleanor Rathbone. The Labour Party was also separately represented on the Basque Children's Committee, which, for the sake of maintaining the appearance of political impartiality, appointed one MP from each party as an Honorary Secretary. Other than the Duchess of Atholl, the aristocracy was represented on the National Joint Committee by the Earl of Listowel, who often took the Chair in its early days, and Lady Young, and on the Basque Children's Committee by Viscount Cecil of Chelwood who was the Honorary Treasurer.

Wilfrid Roberts was a tall, thin man of thirty-seven who in 1935 had been elected Liberal MP for North Cumberland, a constituency he was to serve for the next fifteen years. Wealthy parents and a public school education followed by Oxford set him in the mould of many leading young figures of the twenties and thirties. He was an ardent supporter of the Republican side in the Spanish Civil War and also involved in the Peace Movement.

David Rhys Grenfell was the Labour MP for the Gower Division of Glamorgan, a seat he was to hold until 1959. The son of a coal miner, he had gone to work underground at the age of twelve and had slowly worked his way up to colliery manager. In 1916 he was appointed a miners' agent and in 1922 entered Parliament for the first time. A successful political career, including serving on the Forestry Commission, the Royal Commission on Safety in Mines and the Welsh Land Settlement Commission, left him less time to devote to the Basques than was the case for Wilfrid Roberts but he was, nevertheless, an active participant at many committee meetings and particularly involved with the home set up for boys in Carmarthenshire.

A number of remarkable women served on the two committees. Katharine, Duchess of Atholl, was a woman in her early sixties when the Spanish Civil War broke out. Born into an aristocratic family who had been the lairds of Banff since 1232, she married the future Duke of Atholl in 1899 and, with no children, devoted herself to good causes. During the 1914-18 War, she turned the family seat, Blair Castle, into an auxiliary hospital and, when the Second World War broke out, she again put the family home to good use, this time to take in evacuee children. She had the distinction of being the first woman MP for Scotland, winning in 1923 the Kinross and West Perthshire seat, which her husband had held until 1917, and the first Conservative woman Minister, having been appointed Under Secretary of State to the Board of Education in 1924.

The Duchess was a woman of strong convictions, not determined by party allegiance. She resigned the Party Whip over policies in India and in 1938 she resigned her seat, losing the subsequent by-election, which she fought in support of Churchill and re-armament. Totally opposed to any form of totalitarianism, the 'Red Duchess' was as voluble in her support of East European refugees after the Second World War as she was in her support for the Basque Children and other refugees from the Spanish conflict.

On the other side of the domestic political fence stood Ellen Wilkinson. The third of four children from a Methodist home in Manchester, she won a scholarship to Manchester University in 1910 where she studied history. Her passion, however, was politics. First involved with the women's suffrage movement and then trades unionism in Manchester, Ellen Wilkinson was a founder member of the British Communist Party but she left it in 1924 and became Labour MP for Middlesbrough East in the same year. She lost her seat in 1931 but returned to the Commons in 1935 as MP for Jarrow. She marched in the Jarrow Crusade in 1936. A member of the National Government during the Second World War, Ellen Wilkinson was appointed Minister of Education in the 1945 Labour Government but died at the comparatively early age of 56 in 1947. There can be no doubt about where her sympathies lay in the Spanish Civil War.

The other truly outstanding female politician to be involved with the Basque Children's cause was Eleanor Rathbone. Born in 1872 into a prominent Liverpool family of Quaker origins, Eleanor Rathbone went up to Somerville College, Oxford in 1893 where she proved to be an exceptional student, particularly in philosophy. The academic life, however, did not interest her and she returned to Liverpool, where she carried out a number of sociological studies including, *How the Casual Labourer Lives* in 1909 and *The Conditions of Widows under the Poor Law in Liverpool* in 1913. She was involved in the women's suffrage movement in the 1890s and in 1929 became an Independent MP for the Combined English Universities, the only woman to stand successfully without the backing of a party machine.

Numerous relief committees were represented on the National Joint Committee, ranging from the highly respected Save the Children Fund to more obscure voluntary groups such as the Women's Committee against War and Fascism or the University Ambulance Unit. The Spanish Civil War clearly afforded a tremendous opportunity for philanthropic and politically inclined people to 'get involved'; it was also apparent that most of the groups that sprang up as a direct consequence of the conflict in Spain were left-wing and tended to support the Republican side. The relief work done by the Quakers was a notable exception to this rule.

Representatives of the medical world included the two doctors, Ellis and Russell, who had examined the children in Bilbao, and Dame Janet Campbell who was a pioneering medical reformer and expert in obstetrics and child welfare. She was a founder member of the Medical Women's Federation and had acted as a Medical Officer to the Board of Education as well as Senior Medical Officer in charge of maternal and child welfare until 1934, when she had to resign following her marriage to Michael Heseltine, the Registrar of the British Medical Register. Created Dame of the British Empire in 1924, Dame Janet's international standing and non-political involvement in the problems of childcare made her an invaluable asset to the Basque Children's Committee.

Edith Pye, by profession a midwife, was the most regular attendee from the Society of Friends and from her contributions at meetings and various letters emerges as one of the few truly non-political voices on the committees. Both the Salvation Army and the Roman Catholic church were initially represented on the Basque Children's Committee. The Catholic representative was Canon George Craven, appointed by Cardinal Hinsley, the Archbishop of Westminster, because of his long experience in running the Crusade of Rescue and Homes for Destitute Catholic Children.

Of the people comprising these committees it could be said, however, that most were amateurs in the field of relief work. Some had direct experience of working in refugee camps, such as WH Sams who was appointed to set up the Southampton camp, or were experts in a relevant field, such as Dr Norman White who for some years was the chief of the epidemiological department at the League of Nations. Not a few, on the other hand, were politicians or strongly motivated politically to the extent that their political views tended to cloud their objectivity, particularly when it came to the thorny problem of repatriation of the children.

These committees were not small: twenty or more people would regularly attend the meetings. A relatively small nucleus of people tended to dominate the meetings and effectively take the decisions but, nevertheless, the sheer number of people who had to be consulted made the Committees unwieldy instruments to manage and this may, at least in part, explain the proliferation of smaller sub-committees of the main ones. In this context, it is interesting to note the various off-shoot groupings which were created in the first five months alone of the Basque Children's Committee's operation:

- Finance and General Purposes Committee
- Centres Committee (to evaluate in detail the offers made to accommodate the children at various centres)
- Ad hoc committee to cope with offers of help
- Medical Sub-Committee
- Clothing Sub-Committee

The officers of the National Joint Committee automatically belonged to the Basque Children's Committee and, other than the Earl of Listowel, occupied identical positions on each. The Chairman of both was the Duchess of Atholl and the three MPs - Grenfell, MacNamara and Roberts - were Honorary Secretaries. Vice Chairmen of the National Joint Committee were the Earl of Listowel and Eleanor Rathbone MP while for the Basque Children's Committee Miss Rathbone and Victor Tewson of the TUC filled the position. While Wilfrid Roberts acted as Honorary Treasurer of the National Joint Committee, the Basque Children's Committee was able to secure Viscount Cecil of Chelwood for this nominal post.

The political prejudices of the members of the Committees were to become most apparent when the vexed question of repatriation of the children was raised for the first time and then continued to be raised over a number of years. At a meeting of the National Joint Committee on 9 June a letter was read out from the Friends Service Council, complaining that speakers at a meeting in the Queen's Hall had expressed political views as though they were the official views of the Committee. The Society of Friends felt unable to cooperate with the Committee if it were connected with the politics of the Civil War rather than the relief work. The solution agreed by the Committee was a suitably political compromise - namely, that a statement would be read at the beginning of every meeting stressing the impartiality of the Committee but at the same time admitting the right of speakers to express their individual views of the political situation.

The relationship between the National Joint Committee and the Basque Children's Committee was not clearly established at the beginning. At first, the National Joint Committee set up a sub-committee on 5 May to deal with the evacuation of the as yet unspecified number of children. The members of this committee were the officers of the National Joint Committee, Dame Janet Campbell, Mr Norman White and representatives of the Save the Children Fund, Society of Friends, the Archbishop of Westminster, the TUC and the Spanish Medical Aid Committee. On 26 May this sub-committee was given full power to act in any emergency. When the Basque Children's Committee met for the first time on 31 May, the members present agreed unanimously that they were not a sub-committee of the National Joint Committee and set up their own bank account to channel funds exclusively towards the care of the children.

The Basque Children's Committee accepted 'complete responsibility financially and otherwise' for the Basque children in England, according to a letter from Sir John Simon, the Home Secretary, and this included 'responsibility for repatriation as soon as conditions permitted.' Although the National Joint Committee reviewed the activities of the Basque Children's Committee at its meetings, it was generally content for the Basque Children's Committee to take the decisions as far as homes and general maintenance or welfare of the children were concerned.

When the problem of repatriation became increasingly public and politicised, the National Joint Committee did step in to some extent but it is clear that the National Joint Committee's concerns were far wider than those of the Basque Children's Committee, since it was busy co-ordinating relief action in Spain and in setting up homes or 'colonias' for refugees in both Spain and France. It had limited time to devote to the everyday problems facing the Basque Children's Committee. When repatriation was causing difficulties publicly in October 1937, the National Joint Committee asked their Organising Secretary, Mrs Miller, to look into the constitutional relationship between the National Joint Committee and the Basque Children's Committee. Not surprisingly, she reported back that the situation was unclear and the National Joint Committee let the matter drop. From then on, however, most public announcements on the repatriation question were issued jointly by both committees.

Thirteen organisations sat on the National Joint Committee:
Save the Children Fund
Spanish Medical Aid
Spanish Youth Foodship Committee
Holborn Committee of Medical Aid
Committee against Malnutrition
Friends of Spain Committee
Council of Action
Women's Committee against War and Fascism
Spanish Women's Committee for Help to Spain
League of Nations Union
International Committee for Relief of Victimised Teachers
University Ambulance Unit
Friends Service Council

Just eight organisations sat on the Basque Children's Committee:
Salvation Army
Save the Children Fund
Society of Friends
Crusade of Rescue (Roman Catholic Church)

Labour Party
T.U.C.
Spanish Medical Aid
The Society of Friends

Prominent on both the National Joint Committee and the Basque Children's Committee was the Society of Friends. In keeping with their humanitarian stand against war and for the need to help innocent victims of violence, the Friends, or Quakers, began early in 1937 to organise relief work in Spain in the form of distribution of essentials such as milk, cod liver oil and clothing. They joined with the other organisations then active in Spain in sending volunteers to work there and in raising money at home.

Such Quaker activity was channelled primarily through the Friends' Service Council (FSC). Throughout 1937, the Quaker weekly, *The Friend*, ran articles about the relief work carried out in Spain. As early as January, Barrington Whitlow pointed out in a letter that, 'Friends are taking active steps with the 'Save the Children Fund' to alleviate the suffering caused in Spain', while in June an article by Alfred Jacob noted that there had been Quaker activity for some six months in Spain, through the FSC, the Save the Children Fund and the International Union, involving, among other things, the operation of five canteens in Barcelona alone. Many Quaker volunteers went out to Spain during this period including Edith Pye, Cuthbert Wigham, Alfred Jacob and Esther Farquhar.

The Quakers, with their pacifist beliefs, had difficulties reconciling their advocacy of inaction over such things as air raids with the suffering caused by the bombing of civilians in Spain, on a scale far greater than had been seen hitherto. The debate continued throughout 1937 on whether or not it was possible, or even right, to take defensive action against air raids. The usefulness of gas masks and air raid shelters was questioned, while the moral responsibility for the escalation in deaths of women, children and non-combatants was laid firmly at the door of post-World War I diplomacy (*The Friend,* 4 June).

As well as in Barcelona and Madrid, the Friends were active in the

Basque Country and sent back reports on conditions in Bilbao in late April. In the 23 April issue of *The Friend*, the idea of removing children from the theatre of war is first mentioned: a Spanish woman is quoted as saying, 'Take our children away. Save them at least from the horrors of this war.' After Guernica, on 26 April, the reaction of the Quakers was much as others, 'The reports of the destruction of Guernica have aroused universal condemnation amongst thoughtful people.' The Quaker leadership, however, was unwilling to acknowledge the usefulness of taking children out of the country, preferring a policy of attempting to set up refuges for them in other parts of Spain. Cuthbert Wigham was 'doubtful of the wisdom of evacuating the Basque children to England' while a letter from Dr Richard Ellis about the evacuation of the children was prefaced by a statement that the Quakers believed the children were best helped in their own country.

Not all Quakers were of the same opinion, however, and a number, including Edith Pye, were prominent in the work of the Basque Children's Committee. In the 11 June issue of *The Friend* she makes the point that although people in Spain would undoubtedly agree that it would be best for the children if they could stay, conditions in Bilbao were impossible while in many parts of Republican Spain there was no organised religion, which was a major problem for the large majority of Basques who were devoutly religious.

Once the Basque children came to England, many Meetings raised money or even ran homes for some of the children. Bournville people were already preparing a home in Offenham in June, while the Meeting at Street took on responsibility for forty children. Yet another group, the Leeds Meeting, raised money through Flag Days for the children, once raising funds, somewhat ironically, for these victims of war on the occasion of a military tattoo.

Thus, although the Quakers at the official level might not have approved of the removal of the children from their native country, the ordinary members of Meeting Houses throughout England were active in supporting the children. Certain individual Quakers ended by adopting some of the children and stayed in close touch, ever ready to support them, when in need, for the rest of their lives.

Chapter Eight

Repatriation and the Church

'When are these Basques returning?'

(Mother Superior, Leyfield Schools, Liverpool)

It was not long before the question of whether the children could be returned to Spain was raised, both publicly in the press and within the confines of the Basque Children's Committee. At a meeting on 5 July, it was noted that the Catholic newspaper *The Universe* had printed a report concerning a certain Mr Sturrup who was said to represent General Franco. Sturrup had stated that the authorities in Spain were ready to receive the children (Bilbao had fallen to the insurgent Nationalists a fortnight previously) and that the Roman Catholics in the UK were anxious and willing to take the children back but were not being allowed to do so. The Basque Children's Committee had invited Sturrup to two meetings but he had failed to turn up to either.

Captain MacNamara noted that he had received a lot of enquiries concerning the question of repatriation and that it was essential that the Committee decide what its policy should be. Among other things, he suggested that the Committee should set up an office in Bilbao to process requests for the return of children. The Duchess of Atholl disagreed and, perhaps for that reason, the proposal made no further headway at the meeting. The Committee did agree to the repatriation of individual children, provided that the father or guardian made an appropriate declaration before the Basque Delegation in Paris or through a British Consul and that the relative(s) involved met the expenses involved in transferring the particular child. The Committee does not appear at this stage to have considered how it was going to make known these conditions to the parents concerned.

A press statement was also agreed to the effect that the Committee was acting as the children's 'temporary guardian' and that conditions were still unsettled in Spain. The Committee's decision to place itself effectively 'in loco parentis' was to cause problems in the future with the Church as was the question of whether or not conditions in Spain were sufficiently normal for the children to return. The concern expressed by MacNamara marked the beginning of a battle between, on the one hand, himself and Canon Craven, the Archbishop of Westminster's representative, and, on the other, most of the other members of the Committee, over the question of the repatriation of the children.

If the Committee was, by and large, unwilling just yet to repatriate the children, the problem of what to do with certain of the older, rather wild boys soon forced their hand. Trouble at Stoneham, with a number of the boys throwing stones and rioting, was sufficiently alarming for seventy of them to be transferred to a colony in Carmarthenshire within a matter of days. According to the reports made at the 20 July meeting of the Basque Children's Committee, some of these boys had clearly criminal tendencies while others were really mental cases. The rumours that had started to circulate concerning these boys' behaviour were adversely affecting the fund-raising by committees, particularly in the Southampton area and round Carmarthen. There had also been a widely reported incident at the camp in Scarborough when the cook had been chased by the boys; of these, six had been sent for a short time to an English Boys Hostel at Carlisle. In addition to the effect on fund-raising, the physical damage that had been done at both Carmarthen and Scarborough was substantial and was the liability of the Basque Children's Committee.

It is clear that the Committee could not handle adequately the problem of these older boys. At Stoneham, the Borstal association had kindly offered the services of some officers but they could not speak Spanish - which hindered considerably their efforts at enforcing a stricter discipline on the wayward adolescents. Frightened at losing yet more potential funds through the bad publicity created by the boys, the Committee decided that something had to be done very fast. It was suggested at first that the fifteen most difficult boys should be returned to Spain as soon as possible; so soon, in fact, that there would be no time to inform their parents. This number was increased to a final twenty-three, fifteen from Wales and eight from Stoneham. Canon Craven urged that the boys be sent back only in accordance of the wishes of the Basque Delegation in London - whether they were consulted is not apparent but the boys were sent back to a boys' hostel run in Catalonia by the American Association of Friends. Alfred Jacobs of the Friends' Service Council, who was in Spain, was to be given a watching brief over the boys.

Thus, although the Committee tended to resist sending back other children, they moved extremely quickly to remove from England the most troublesome of the older boys, perhaps the very children who needed the most help. That they were prepared to send back these boys without the permission of their parents and to a different part of Spain from the one from which they had come serves to underline the inconsistencies of the Committee members' attitudes. On the other hand, to have kept the boys would have increased the dangers of adverse publicity in the press, some sections of which were only too pleased to be able to represent the children as Reds and uncontrollable criminals who should never have been allowed into the country in the first place. To preserve the majority, the few had to go.

In the meantime, the Foreign Office was becoming concerned about the repatriation of the children and Eden wrote to the Committee, making two important suggestions. The first was that they should provide the insurgent authorities in Bilbao with a list of the children, inviting them to cooperate in tracing the parents; the second was that the Committee should send its own representative to Bilbao to explore the situation at first hand. Lord Cecil of Chelwood and Canon Craven were in favour of complying with the Foreign Secretary's requests. The rest of the Committee were unanimously against sending a list to the insurgents.

Wilfrid Roberts played a key role in persuading the Committee against such a move, arguing that no official requests for the return of children had been received from parents in Bilbao and that no valid authority had yet approached the Committee asking for the children to be returned. Evidence was produced of the possibility of coercion on the parents, namely a boy in Theydon Bois had received a letter from his parents saying that he should return home and join the Black Arrows (an insurgent outfit). The boy had pointed out a tear in the corner of the letter, which he said was a pre-arranged signal to disregard the contents of any letter so marked. Lord Listowel remarked that from previous experience it was likely that the victorious side would exert pressure on the parents for the return of their children.

The 20 July meeting of the Committee decided against sending a list to the insurgents and in favour of sending a delegation to Bilbao. In addition, it was also agreed that Wilfrid Jones of the American Society of Friends, who was in Bilbao at the time, should be contacted to find out about conditions then prevailing in the Basque Country.

During August, the opposition of the Roman Catholic Church to the way the Committee was approaching the question of repatriation grew substantially. On 17 August, Canon Craven wrote to Roberts urging that repatriation be speeded up, 'On the word of the Delegate on the spot (the Pope's Apostolic Delegate) the conditions laid down by the Committee for the repatriation of these children - the wishes of parents and safety - are now fulfilled.' The Archbishop of Westminster, Hinsley, also wrote to Roberts with details of the Special Commission sent by the Holy See to Bilbao to enquire into conditions there and noted that the parents lacked information on the whereabouts of their children. In the Archbishop's view it was necessary to obtain full information on the names of the children, their places of refuge and their places of origin. On 18 August, a notice was published in *The Catholic Herald* asking for information on the Basque children to be sent to the Apostolic Delegate in Bilbao.

One of the reasons why the Catholic Church in Britain may have been keener than others for the children to go back was the tremendous financial burden it was facing as it had undertaken the care of some 1,200 of the children. However, another factor that cannot be ignored was the attitude of the Holy See to the two protagonists in the war. Argument within the Church had been lively, at the very least, as to which if either side was in the right from a theological viewpoint. Although the priests in the Basque Country tended to support the Republican struggle against the Nationalists, the Papacy inclined increasingly towards the Nationalists, particularly in the wake of widely reported killings of priest, monks, nuns and other religious in the Republican-held territories.

On 1 July, the Spanish hierarchy published a joint letter to 'The Bishops of the Whole World' in which they argued that thousands of Christians had 'taken up arms on their personal responsibility to save the principles of religion', that those in power since 1931 had endeavoured to change 'Spanish history in a way contrary to the needs of the national spirit' and that the Comintern had armed 'a revolutionary militia to seize power'. In the Spanish Bishops' view the insurgents' cause was theologically justifiable and they reprimanded the Basque priests for not having listened to 'the voice of the Church'. Not all the Spanish establishment supported this view, notable dissenters being the Archbishop of Tarragona and the Bishop of Vitoria. The latter argued that true religious freedom in the Nationalist-held territory did not exist and that death sentences were being carried out there without trial. The Basque priests, however, were accused of having borne arms and acted as politicians; the Bishop of Vitoria denied these charges to no avail. On August 28 the Vatican recognised the Nationalists, with their headquarters at Burgos, as the official Government of Spain and from then on any Catholic who sided with the Republican cause, or even stayed neutral, was viewed as a traitor to the Papacy.

The support for Franco from the Church percolated through to the convents and Catholic homes where some of the Basque children were being looked after and, in a letter of 27 August, Betty Arne, one of the Joint Organising Secretaries of the Basque Children's Committee, outlined to Wilfrid Roberts some examples of the problems to which this was giving rise. She quoted an extract from a letter from the Mother Superior at Leyfield Schools, West Derby, Liverpool where 31 children were in care, 'I really have not the time for all this correspondence for Basque children. I have sufficient to do with the regard to the business of the school. When are these Basques returning? It is a pity that they were ever brought to this country.'

There also seemed to be a problem at the Honor Oak convent in Birmingham where, Betty Arne had been told, 'the nuns in charge are Italians and all keen Fascists'. The nuns were putting notes into the children's letters to their parents, asking that they, the parents, should ask for their children back. Six of the girls had already been told that they would have to return to their parents 'immediately'.

In the light of the correspondence from the Archbishop of Westminster and other developments, the officers of the Basque Children's Committee geared themselves up for a difficult meeting of the Committee on 31 August. Betty Arne found time to draw up a draft policy outline suggesting that strongly-worded denials be issued concerning the Committee's preventing children from being repatriated but re-emphasising that the Committee would only send back children when their parents had asked for them. She put forward proposals for the mechanics of how a parent might authenticate his request for the return of a child and also suggested that, where the parents were themselves refugees, they should not be required to pay for the children's return expenses as had been decided previously. Not for public consumption was the recommendation that non-Roman Catholic colonies should be circularised to ask them to censor all incoming letters to the children since 'the centres where there is now least trouble, e.g. Brechfa, Scarborough, Camberley, are all doing this, and those in charge report that endless trouble has been stopped as a result.'

Roberts wrote to the Archbishop before the meeting suggesting that closer contacts should be maintained between the various centres and organisations dealing with refugees.

Canon Craven did not attend the 31 August meeting but sent a letter to the Committee asking for the names and addresses of children in Catholic homes, the names and addresses of their parents and the names of the places in Spain from which they had come. At the meeting, reservations were expressed concerning the authenticity of reported requests from parents for their children (Sturrup was now claiming that he had a list of 2,000 names of parents wanting the return of their children). The Honor Oak example was quoted as was the fear of returning expressed by some of the children themselves who, it was stated, were 'terrified at the prospect of returning to the Basque country, although some have said they would not mind going to Catalonia'.

It was agreed that two conditions had to be fulfilled for the repatriation of the children - the war risks had to be minimised and the wishes of parents ascertained. There was little disagreement that the first condition had been met but for the second to be fulfilled it was felt that a delegation would have to go to Bilbao. Meanwhile, the extent of the Committee's concerns over the existing lists of parents allegedly claiming their offspring would be placed before the Archbishop in full and Canon Craven would be referred to the Archbishop. Father George, who had attended in Father Craven's place, agreed to these proposals. Neither MacNamara nor Lord Cecil attended the meeting.

Aside from the Catholic question, progress had been made on other fronts - Viscount Cranborne (Parliamentary Under Secretary of State at the Foreign Office) had agreed that the British Consul in Bilbao should counter-sign requests from parents for their children and had also accepted that no list of the children, such as suggested in Eden's earlier letter, should be sent to Spain for the time being. The American Society of Friends had also undertaken to investigate the situation in Spain, although this would have to await the arrival in Europe of a new representative of the Society, expected to reach England on 10 September.

As to the composition of any delegation to Bilbao, it was clear that its members would have to have impeccable credentials as far as their non-alignment politically speaking was concerned. Names were to be submitted to Miss Arne for consideration by the Committee. Meanwhile, the officers were left with the task of drafting a suitable letter to the Archbishop.

At least two drafts were made. The first (possibly drawn up by Betty Arne) was by far the less emotive in the arguments it raised and the cooler in its judgement that the conditions in Bilbao did now meet the requirement that war risks should be minimised prior to the return of the children. A comparison of the way this first obstacle to repatriation is dealt with in the earlier and then the final draft is illuminating. In the first draft, the writer states:

'large numbers of letters are constantly received by the children themselves from their parents, showing that a very large proportion of the parents are aware of where their children are, but these letters do not contain specific requests that the children should return... My Committee is aware that very large numbers of parents left Bilbao before its capture and went to the neighbourhood of Santander. These will now doubtless be returning to their permanent homes and, in view also of the capture of Santander, my Committee feels that the danger of war conditions in Bilbao and neighbourhood is very considerably minimised and that therefore, from this point of view, the possibility of an early return of children is made more possible.'

In the letter that was actually sent to the Archbishop similar thoughts are expressed rather differently:

'I can assure you that my Committee recognise that the war risks in Bilbao are much less than formerly, and are anxious to return the children to their parents whenever we are satisfied that the parents desire this... the fact that large numbers of letters are continually being received by the children themselves from the parents show that a very large proportion of the latter are aware of where their children are. If, seeing that fighting has ceased in Bilbao since June, they do not express in these letters a desire for their children's return, as is the case, it hardly looks as if they felt that conditions were yet quite suitable for this...

'...very large numbers of persons left Bilbao for Santander before Bilbao was taken... Some of these may now be returning to Bilbao. Others may be very difficult to trace. And I am sure your Grace will agree that we have to be very careful to protect the children committed to our care from the danger of being handed over to people who are not their parents or guardians, and who may use them for their private ends.'

The letter sent to the Archbishop was sealed by this appeal: 'Finally, we hear that some children of parents who are opposed to the insurgents, as we believe most of the parents are, have been expressing themselves strongly against being sent back to be under insurgent rule. It is actually feared that if sent against their will, some might try to throw themselves overboard.'

MacNamara, who was in Italy at the time of the 31 August meeting, sent Roberts a letter, received around 4 September, in which he expounded his views on the need to resolve the repatriation question. Most importantly, MacNamara emphasised that repatriation should be carried out by the Basque Children's Committee through its own 'mediums' i.e. not in conjunction with any other countries but as far as possible in direct contact with the parents concerned. He felt sure that, if the Committee acted quickly on the question, the whole project would be considered as a success by outsiders and it would be easier to raise money for other humanitarian ventures. He did not believe this would be the case if the children were all kept on in Britain through the winter. It would not seem, however, that MacNamara's fellow committee members felt the same sense of urgency over the question.

At a meeting of the Executive Committee of the Basque Children's Committee on 20 September, it was noted that there had been interviews with both Sturrup and Father Gabana, the official representative of the Apostolic Delegate, who had made available a card index of parents requesting the return of their children. MacNamara and Craven proposed that the children on Gabana's list (other than those for whom the information was inaccurate) accompany the proposed delegation to Bilbao as an act of good faith. No decision was taken, pending confirmation that the delegation could go ahead.

A National Joint Committee followed immediately after and at this it was noted that Father Gabana had presented applications from 600 parents for 850 children. 'Certain discrepancies' were being investigated and any decision on repatriation was again accordingly deferred.

A special emergency meeting of the Basque Children's Committee and the National Joint Committee convened on 1 October, following a motion submitted by MacNamara and Canon Craven that 'the children on Father Gabana's list be immediately repatriated.'

The Executive Committee meeting of the Basque Children's Committee began at 10am on Friday 1 October. At around 1pm the Basque Children's Committee meeting became a joint one with the National Joint Committee who continued after 2.30pm as the National Joint Committee alone. Altogether, some five hours were devoted to the vexing problem of whether or not to accede to Father Gabana's request - as reflected in the motion.

Lord Cecil of Chelwood was not present neither was Mrs Manning but she was represented by Mr Geoffrey Bing from Spanish Medical Aid. This organisation was further represented by Dr Morgan. The TUC had not only Mr Tewson but also Mr E P Harries. The Labour Party's Chief Woman Officer, Miss Sutherland, also attended as did Colonel Gordon (Salvation Army), Edith Pye (Friends' Service Council), both Wilfrid Roberts and his wife, and a couple of individual members, Miss Todd and Mrs Wood. As well as the movers of the motion, Lord Listowel and the Duchess (in the Chair), also invited were Father Gabana, Dr Norman White and Señor Uranga (the representative of the Spanish (Republican) Government in London). From the outset, the constitution of the committee was unlikely to be favourably disposed towards the motion since those attending were predominantly left-wing or, at a minimum, highly suspicious of the intentions of the Insurgent authorities.

The battle-lines were drawn from the beginning. Tewson questioned the constitutionality of the meeting, in the light of the decision taken previously, and then maintained that there were sufficient discrepancies in Father Gabana's list to throw the whole list into question. In his view, it was essential that repatriation take place in an ordered manner and that the Committee maintain control over the system of repatriation instituted (in other words, he was concerned that the Church might take the question over completely).

The Chairman read to the meeting a letter from the Foreign Office, confirming their view that permission for a delegation to go to Bilbao was unlikely to be accorded by Salamanca (seat of the Nationalist powers) but noting that Father Gabana had suggested that a delegation might be acceptable if it were to accompany the children on his list. Both MacNamara and Craven repeated their conviction that the children should be returned as quickly as possible.

As was often the case, it was the genuinely non-political Edith Pye who suggested a possible compromise. She proposed that the Committee should first consider the 493 children on the Apostolic Delegate's list about whom no discrepancies had been found and she offered the services of two representatives of the Friends' Committee who were now in Burgos. The Duchess was grateful for the offer but wondered whether they would be able to devote sufficient of their time to a detailed investigation of each request, this being the intention of the delegation should it be allowed to go to Spain.

Before Father Gabana was called in to the meeting, Mr Bing suggested that the Committee submit all requests, disputed or not, to an independent tribunal of a judicial nature. No vote was taken on this proposal immediately, which is not surprising since it was the first time that the idea had been put forward. It is very possible that Bing and Mrs Manning had devised this proposal before the meeting as a means of delaying any decision on repatriation. This seems all the more likely given Mrs Manning's violent opposition to the Franco regime and her personal identification with the evacuation of the children in the first place.

When Father Gabana was called in he was subjected to a barrage of questions concerning the validity of the requests from parents that he had brought over from Bilbao. Although he at first maintained that the requests had been given to him personally by the parents at his office, he later admitted that about half the names on the list had been submitted by the Falangist Representatives in Bilbao and half by the Apostolic Delegate's office. He could not recall how many parents he had personally interviewed. He confirmed his belief that if the children requested on the list were returned to Bilbao accompanied by a delegation, then the Salamanca (Nationalist) authorities would create no further difficulties. He suggested that a Joint Office (presumably run by the Apostolic Delegate's office and the Basque Children's Committee) could then also be set up in Bilbao. Additionally, he undertook to compare his card index with the original letters from the parents and the Basque Children's Committee's own lists.

Bing managed to intervene with his suggestion of a tribunal to examine the applications and compare the handwriting of parents in their letters to children with that in the petitions. Somewhat surprisingly, Gabana agreed to this suggestion, provided that the tribunal worked quickly. Bing expanded on the idea of the tribunal to the point where he maintained that each case should be individually examined on its own merits. In his view the children had rights, which meant that they should not be extradited (his word) without their consent. This was, of course, putting even more qualifications on the situations in which a child would be repatriated, far beyond the original remit of the Committee.

Political questions aimed at discovering the Apostolic Delegate's view of the proposed delegation to Bilbao were avoided by Gabana as was the suggestion that he could use his influence to get the representatives accepted without the children. He was firm, however, that he was acting as the representative of the Apostolic Delegate and not as a representative of Franco. By this point in the discussion, both MacNamara and Craven began to show their impatience with the Committee. Canon Craven protested at the political questioning of Father Gabana and urged that the Apostolic Delegate's list be accepted without question. Captain MacNamara stated, more pragmatically, that the committee needed to go some way towards meeting Gabana's proposals, otherwise any further requests for help would undoubtedly be refused.

Before leaving the meeting, Father Gabana agreed to give an independent tribunal all the information at his disposal and to cooperate with it in its work. If a preliminary list of children were arrived at, he undertook to consult with the Nationalist authorities in London to see whether this would be acceptable.

Once Father Gabana had left the meeting, it was generally agreed that the forty-seven requests for repatriation of children forwarded by the Foreign Office should be dealt with first. Canon Craven, however, stated clearly that the Catholic Church in Britain wanted all the children to go back as soon as possible and, in particular, the children in the Church's care should be sent back immediately, without waiting for a tribunal. He pointed out that if the Committee did not act soon, the Church might be forced to act on its own. Certainly, the Church had been shouldering a significant financial burden in looking after over one thousand of the children and Miss Pye suggested that the Basque Children's Committee might be able to help by taking on the costs of some of the children.

Most of the discussion, however, was concerned with the difficult problem of who should compose the tribunal or Commission or Repatriation Committee, the names variously suggested for its title. MacNamara felt it important to keep the goodwill of Father Gabana who was, in his opinion, 'the most reasonable of all the authorities' with whom the Basque Children's Committee were likely to have to deal. The rest of the Committee did not share his view and it was Mr Tewson's suggestion that the independent Commission should comprise three outside people not connected with either Father Gabana or the Basque Children's Committee.

Captain MacNamara, Canon Craven and Miss Pye did not vote on the proposal. Canon Craven, in particular, made clear his opposition to the creation of the new body and MacNamara was concerned at the possibility of further delays. By this time the members of the National Joint Committee had joined the meeting and Mrs Brown reiterated the point made at the previous meeting of the National Joint Committee that had so concerned MacNamara, namely that the National Joint Committee had borne the greatest financial responsibility and, therefore, had the ultimate responsibility in the repatriation question. The Basque Children's Committee members not on the National Joint Committee and Captain MacNamara left the meeting and the National Joint Committee formally endorsed the decision by the Basque Children's Committee to set up the tribunal. However, the question of the constitutional relationship of the two committees was raised (and deferred pending investigations) thus reflecting the concern of some members that they should assert greater control in this sensitive area of sending the children back to Nationalist-held Bilbao.

Both movers of the original motion that had prompted the calling of the meeting wrote letters immediately afterwards, MacNamara to Roberts and the Canon to the Duchess. In his letter, MacNamara explained that he had absented himself from the National Joint Committee meeting because he felt that that committee did not have jurisdiction over the Basque Children's Committee and should not, therefore, discuss the repatriation question. Furthermore, the Duchess in her letter to him had implied that she would deal with the National Joint Committee on this question and he did not wish to speak behind her back. (The Duchess had had to leave the Basque Children's Committee meeting before the end.) His other concern was that the Basque Children's Committee had to act on repatriation before the Roman Catholics did so on their own. As MacNamara put it, rather neatly, 'The committee must realise that there are two points of view and that others have to be considered besides those who only read through left wing spectacles.'

While MacNamara was still hoping for an amicable resolution of the question, Canon Craven now held out very little hope of the Committee's reaching a decision that would satisfy the Church; 'I am forced now to consult my Archbishop to ask him what shall be my next step as it is only too clear to me that every possible difficulty is being placed by yourself and one or two others on the Committee in the way of repatriation.'

The Canon's formal letter of resignation, on the instructions of his Archbishop, arrived four days later. He really had no option. The Committee had refused to accept a list presented by the Apostolic Delegate's representative, which, according to that authority, had already been presented and approved by the British Ambassador at Hendaye and the Consul at Bilbao. By questioning the validity of Father Gabana's requests, the Committee had made it plain that they trusted neither the man's lists nor the man himself. Furthermore, in Craven's own words the Committee had now decided to 'submit the names on these lists to three strangers. That is to say, you prefer the word of three people who know nothing at all about the question, nothing at all about the circumstances of those who make the requests, to the word of the Apostolic Delegate who is on the spot in Bilbao.' Canon Craven's position, in the light of these clear attacks on the integrity of the Church, was untenable.

Roberts accepted the Canon's resignation with regret but pointed out that the Foreign Office could not confirm that their representatives on the scene had approved Father Gabana's lists. He was also concerned about how the Committee could continue to exercise its responsibility towards the children in the Catholic homes without a representative of the Church on the Committee. In this respect, he pointed out that Catholic authorities in other countries were not showing themselves as keen as the British to repatriate the children in their care.

Canon Craven was not moved by Wilfrid Roberts's arguments but contact was maintained between the Basque Children's Committee and the Church over the children in Catholic homes, albeit from a rather frosty distance and, in the Committee's view, with inadequate information on the standards of care in the Catholic homes, most of which operated outside the orbit of the Basque Children's Committee's network of inspectors and advisers from now on.

Meanwhile, the appointment of three outsiders, notwithstanding the Church's disapproval, proceeded rapidly. The committee was chaired by Sir Holman Gregory, the other two members being Theobald Matthew K.C. and Richard Ludlow, a Ministry of Labour arbitrator. This legal Commission consulted with not just Father Gabana but also Sir Arnold Wilson K.C.I.E., D.S.O., M.P. who was a member of a Basque Children Repatriation Committee, which had been set up at the request of General Franco's representative in London (the Duke of Alba) under the chairmanship of the Duke of Wellington. Discussions were also held with representatives of the Basque Children's Committee and of the Basque Government.

The terms of reference of the legal enquiry were established by the Basque Children's Committee but slightly amended by the National Joint Committee at its meeting on 11 October, evidently in an effort to limit the Commission's enquiries solely to the consideration of the children whose return had allegedly been requested by their parents. The Repatriation Commission, as it was finally called, was empowered to:

- consider the policy with regard to repatriation laid down by the Committee (this being interpreted by the National Joint Committee to mean consider how best the policy with regard to repatriation, as laid down by the Basque Children's Committee and approved by the National Joint Committee, should be carried out)
- advise upon the question of the repatriation of the Basque children in England (qualified by the National Joint Committee to apply only to those children whose repatriation had already been requested)
- consider all the applications which have been made to date for the return of the children to Spain
- recommend which of the applications appeared beyond reasonable doubt to be authentic requests
- to those ends, consult all concerned, in particular Father Gabana.

That the National Joint Committee kept a very close watch on the Commission's activities is beyond doubt; a revealing note to Roberts from G T Garratt, who among other things was closely involved in the running of a National Joint Committee boys' colony in Catalonia, is indicative of the attention which was being paid as well as an insight into the workings of the Commission.

From Garratt's letter, it appears that someone from the National Joint Committee or the Basque Children's Committee sat with Sir Holman Gregory throughout the time that he was examining the petitions that had been signed by parents in Bilbao. Father Gabana was also present for most of the time and, by dint of this enforced closeness, 'the little round fat oily man of God' now greeted Garratt as his long-lost brother. Gregory, on the other hand, did not appear to be the hot-shot that might have been implied by his chairing the Commission, since, in Garratt's opinion, he was 'an old man whose mind has gone quite rusty'. (Gregory, a well-known judge, was 73 years old.)

The main thrust of Garratt's letter was to ensure that either Roberts or the Duchess had to make sure to be present, with an agreed plan of action, when Gregory met with his fellow referees the following weekend. Garratt suggested that the Committee(s) should agree to send back at least those children whose parents were living in Northern Spain and had asked for their return, whether or not under pressure. The fact that many of the petitions appeared to have been produced in offices to a prescribed format would not influence Gregory and, therefore, some kind of compromise would have to be agreed upon if the National Joint Committee and Basque Children's Committee were not to lose credibility.

That Roberts underestimated the likely number of children for whom Gregory would recommend repatriation is clear from a policy note that he sent to Betty Arne shortly after receiving Garratt's information. In this note, Roberts suggests that, if the Commission recommended sending back the one hundred or so children for whom both parents had signed the application, the Committee should not oppose this. Furthermore, for those children of whom only one parent had signed, Roberts believed the best course would be not to oppose their return but to have a pro forma sent to Bilbao which, if properly filled in, could then be used as a basis for returning these children as well. Pollock, at the Foreign Office, agreed that the British Consul in Bilbao could hold such forms and forward them, once completed, but clearly could not act as any kind of arbitrator in the affair.

As it turned out, the Commission completed its work in about ten days and then reported its findings in a report which was considered at a joint meeting of the National Joint Committee and the Basque Children's Committee on 28 October. The main thrust of the Commission's recommendations was that 500 children should go back immediately, accompanied by an English doctor and superintendent, nominated by the Committee. Additionally, the Commission had made the general recommendation that 'all the Spanish children now in Great Britain be returned to their parents or relations or guardians as soon as can conveniently be arranged'.

Few members of the Committee were completely happy with the findings of the Commission but both the Duchess and Wilfrid Roberts, at least, recognised the need to comply as far as possible with the Commission's findings while Captain MacNamara pointed out that in sending back the 500 accompanied by Committee nominees, the Committee's chief concern, that of sending representatives to Bilbao, could be met.

Exception was generally taken to the reference to relations, since the Committee's responsibility was towards parents or guardians only. Concern was also expressed at sending back children of anarchists, communists and others opposed to the Franco regime. No decision was taken on this point but since there were well in excess of 800 children from which to choose the 500, the problem could be resolved in careful selection. The Committee did decide, however, to consult children over the age of fourteen as to whether they wished to return. Additionally, it was also decided that the 500 could not be returned simultaneously since this would make it virtually impossible for checks to be carried out in Bilbao, as was still the intention. The children would be returned in batches.

A Resolution thanking the Commission for its work and acknowledging that the Committee would send back the 500 at the earliest moment practicable was passed and it and the Report were made public. The die had been cast; the repatriation of the children was now to begin in earnest and the first batch, of 160 children, was scheduled to leave for Spain on Friday November 12, accompanied by Dr White and Dame Janet Campbell, Father Gabana and an appropriate number of staff to look after the children. Although it was anticipated that thereafter a regular system for repatriation of the children would have to be set up, the Committee was also very aware of the fact that there were some 3,000 children still in their care and for whom no request had yet been made for their return. The continuing drain on the financial resources of the National Joint Committee and Basque Children's Committee would be great.

Chapter Nine

Pressures in Spain

'Spain receives with joy the children repatriated from England'

(*Gaceta del Norte* - newspaper based in Bilbao)

One of the major concerns of Committee members in England was that the parents of the children who had been evacuated from Bilbao were being placed under unreasonable pressure to ask for the return of their children.

If certain of the guiding lights behind the evacuation were at pains to disclaim the political nature of the act, it is very clear that the Franco regime considered it to have been a deliberately political move aimed against the insurgent Nationalist side in the Civil War. Throughout the second half of 1937, the Nationalist-controlled newspapers in the north of Spain conducted a campaign to urge parents to reclaim their children, in terms which can only be described as threatening. In early July, the *Gaceta del Norte* was describing the evacuation of children from the Basque Country as having been organised in the last months of 'red-separatist' domination before the entry of the glorious nationalist forces. The newspaper claimed that full lists of the children who had been evacuated were available in Santander, implying in this way that it was hopeless for parents to pretend that they had not sent their children away.

However, as late as December the same paper carried a notice urging that people come forward with details of names, dates and places of origin of children who had been evacuated, to facilitate the process of repatriation. Other notices also appeared asking that specified persons go to the Apostolic Delegate's office, on the pretext that their children were seeking information about them. On the basis of evidence from children who were, in fact, in contact with their parents, it would appear that the real purpose behind these notices was to persuade the parents, once they arrived at the office, to ask for the return of their children.

Philip Jordan, who was a supporter of the Republic, quoted in the left-wing British newspaper, the *News Chronicle*, an article which appeared in the *Correo Español* in late August. This had urged, 'Parents must hasten to present their credentials applying officially for the return of their children. Parents who have not asked for their return will bitterly regret not having done so.' That this was the case, in at least some instances, is borne out by the evidence of one of the Basque children who stayed in England.

Helvecia Garcia's father had been a leading Socialist in the small village of Larboleda before the war. Once the Falangist forces had won in the North, Francoist sympathisers broke into the homes of well-known left-wingers and ransacked them, including the home of Helvecia's now widowed mother. Thereafter, she and the few other parents in the neighbourhood who had not asked for the return of their children were subjected to regular public humiliation, being forced on occasion to attend public meetings in the Plaza where the speakers would harangue as traitors to their country those who did not request the return of their children. When the time came for the Fascist salute, there were always people ready to prop up unwilling arms.

An Edict published in August exemplifies the attitude of the central authorities to the evacuation of the children, 'the children in England, Belgium and France ... are being used to denigrate the New Spain, our army and glorious caudillo. The parents of evacuated children must immediately reclaim them, particularly the children in England.' Again, in the *Gaceta del Norte*, the reclamation of the children was characterised as a 'true matter of conscience'. Why the children in England should have seemed so important is not obvious except, perhaps, that their evacuation had received very widespread publicity at the time and they were the only significant group of Spanish refugees in England at the time. For as long as they remained in England, it could be interpreted as though the British authorities were in some way opposed to the Franco regime.

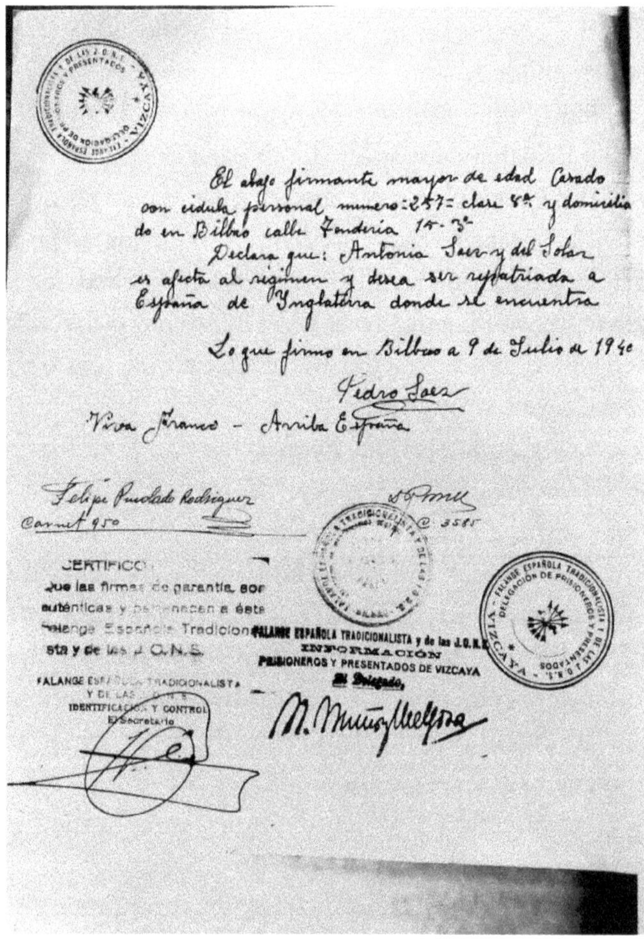

El abajo firmante mayor de edad Casado con cédula personal numero: 257 = clase 8ª y domiciliado en Bilbao calle Fundería 15 - 3º

Declara que: Antonia Saez y del Solar es afecta al régimen y desea ser repatriada a España de Inglaterra donde se encuentra

Lo que firmo en Bilbao a 9 de Julio de 1940

Pedro Saez

Viva Franco - Arriba España

Felipe Puelado Rodriguez
Carnet 950

CERTIFICO:
Que las firmas de garantía son auténticas y pertenecen a esta Falange Española Tradicionalista y de las J.O.N.S.

FALANGE ESPAÑOLA TRADICIONALISTA Y DE LAS J.O.N.S.
IDENTIFICACIÓN Y CONTROL
El Secretario

FALANGE ESPAÑOLA TRADICIONALISTA y de las J.O.N.S.
INFORMACIÓN
PRISIONEROS Y PRESENTADOS DE VIZCAYA
El Delegado,

M. Muñoz Melgosa

Fig 5. An official request in July 1940 for the repatriation from England of Antonia Saez, stating her support of the Francoist regime. Witnessed by a representative of the official Falangist party. Note the Viva Franco – Arriba España below the signature.

When the first batch of children were sent back to Spain, the *Gaceta* was appropriately effusive about their homecoming, 'Spain receives with joy the children repatriated from England..........Father Henry

Gabana recommended to the little ones that when they reached their homes, they should write to England describing the welcome they had received in their homeland...........Today, they were welcomed by the national flag which is the symbol of Catholic Spain.'

The degree to which parents freely asked for the return of their children is open to doubt. Mrs McClintock, who accompanied a party of children to Bilbao late in 1937, reported afterwards to the Foreign Office that food was plentiful, the local authorities had been helpful and she had been allowed to interview parents privately in their own homes. This was an authorised visit, of course, and it seems likely that the parents Mrs McClintock visited had been carefully screened beforehand. Ronald Thackrah, who helped run the Barnet children's home and became increasingly involved in the work of the Basque Children's Committee, had a different tale to tell.

Thackrah went to Spain in 1938 to try and investigate on the spot the validity of certain requests for the return of children. When he arrived at the border town of Hendaye, he had not yet received a safe conduct pass from the Spanish authorities and was uncertain of his next move. Fate was kind, however, in the shape of a high-born Bilbao lady who was staying at the same hotel. She and her husband, who was Irish, had been intending to visit her relatives in Bilbao and two safe conduct passes had been issued to the couple. Unfortunately, the husband had mumps. After some discussion, it was agreed that Thackrah could take over the identity of the lady's husband. They passed the frontier with no problem. At the Bilbao hotel, the delicate question of sleeping quarters was resolved through Thackrah's feigning insomnia and requesting a separate room from his 'wife' so as not to disturb her during the night. They were accordingly given separate rooms.

From his safe base, Thackrah visited the parents he could find and questioned them concerning their requests for the return of their children. He could discover only one genuine request - the others told him that they had been instructed by the local police to ask for their children. Unfortunately, Thackrah had difficulty in locating one of the families, the Antolins who lived in Ortuella, and he had to stop at various houses on the way to ask for directions. The next day the police called at his hotel and checked his papers. He was confined to the hotel and escorted to the frontier the following morning.

Although in these cases, it was clear that pressure had been put on the parents, by the time that Thackrah was again actively involved in the repatriation question, there seems to have been no doubt about the parents' wish to see their children again. In December 1940, Thackrah accompanied a trainload of some 500 children back to Spain, where he saw them reunited with their parents who, not surprisingly, felt that they had not sent their children away from the horrors of one war in order to suffer another. This time, Thackrah was quite satisfied that the requests were genuine.

Over the years, certain individual cases are recorded of parents notifying their children to ignore any efforts to persuade them to return to Spain. For example, a letter from the British Embassy, dated July 30, 1942, refers to another letter from Sr Duenas, the father of two daughters at that time in Yorkshire. This stated that the daughters were on no account to follow any instructions to return to Spain, even if these were signed by both parents. Sr Duenas had just recently been released provisionally from imprisonment and was afraid that pressure might be exerted to force the return of the two girls. In a number of cases, parents did not want their children back, not for political reasons but simply because they could not afford to look after them. This seems to have been the experience of Thackrah when he visited Spain again, as late as 1945.

The repatriation of children from England was used in other countries as a means of trying to persuade the authorities in those countries also to repatriate the children entrusted to their care. The Belgian newspaper, *La Métropole* carried a remarkably distorted story on 12 November 1937,

'Sometimes torn away from their parents, often orphaned, they were directed by the Red authorities of Bilbao, Valencia, Madrid or Barcelona, towards England, Russia, Mexico, France or Belgium.

'Now, however, most of the children ... have heard the paternal call of the National Spanish authorities and of the ecclesiastical hierarchy of their country. And they themselves deeply miss in their hearts the sky and warmth of their country.

'England has hurried to reply to this call ... This is an example worth imitating speedily. These unhappy children who had to leave their country by force must be returned as soon as possible.'

The Basque Government in Exile, in Paris, was greatly concerned at the propaganda successes of the Franco regime in the question of repatriation. In September 1937, Miguel de Uranga wrote to Sr Don Juan Garcia, Consejo de Asistencia Social de Euzkadi (the Basque Country) stressing the urgent need for letters from parents in France stating that they did not want their children to be returned. He also noted that the National Joint Committee had been told to take no decision on the repatriation question without first establishing the opinion of the Basque Government.

Additionally, the Basque Government in Exile issued a lengthy statement concerning the reasons for the repatriation of the children, pointing out that this had taken place not only because of the physical dangers to the children from the war but also because of the dangers, should the Basque Country fall, of reprisals or enforced enlistment in military organisations. The Basque Government also published documents which it claimed proved that petitions for the return of children which had been gathered by the Apostolic Delegate were false, that parents in prison had no choice but to comply with the demand that they ask for their children back, and that the apparent calm in the Basque Country was no guarantee of anything.

By early 1938, the Basques were desperately concerned at the possibility that all the children in England might be returned. So much so that a letter was sent from Paris to the Archbishop of Dax, in the south of France, suggesting that he might write to the Archbishop of Westminster putting forward the idea that the Basque children might be sent to France in view of the difficulties encountered by the English Catholics in raising sufficient money to maintain the children. The Basque Government undertook, of course, to return the children to their parents when these latter claimed them 'en bonne et due forme'.

Nothing came of this suggestion. The children were repatriated, slowly, not just from England but also from the other countries to which they had been sent. Indeed, the French Government announced as early as September 1937 their intention to repatriate all refugees who were a charge on public funds. That repatriation from other countries took as long or longer than it did from Britain is testified to by the announcement in the *Gaceta del Norte* of 23 October 1956 that 461 had been repatriated from Russia.

By November 1937 the first group of children had been sent back, but this did not automatically mean that all the children could go back in an orderly fashion. For some, it was impossible to trace their parents, for others who were now orphaned or whose parents were in prison or in refugee camps in France, it was not feasible to send them back in the short term. The pros and cons of repatriation continued to be debated within the ranks of the Committees dealing with the children in Britain and doubts continued to be expressed over the authenticity of requests for children for quite a time to come. However, while repatriation continued to be a sensitive and public issue, the Basque Children's Committee had to get on with the more practical problems of caring for the many children still under their charge, in some 80 homes scattered throughout the country.

Chapter Ten

Raising Money

'I don't think Basque children alone are going to bring in any real money anywhere at the moment. We have to get it on a broader basis. There is so much real distress among our own children....'

(Mrs Adams, Hon. Sec. Ambleside Hostel Branch)

After the first couple of months of the children's stay in Britain, when the natural sympathy stirred by their plight was fuelled by substantial press coverage and appeals, an almost constant source of concern to the organisers of the National Joint Committee and of the Basque Children's Committee was the raising of sufficient funds to meet the heavy demands of maintenance of the children and, later, the not inconsiderable costs of repatriation.

Apart from the children housed in Catholic homes, usually convents, whose maintenance was taken on by the Church and, initially, some 400 children looked after by the Salvation Army at Clapton, the remainder were looked after in homes ranging in size from barely twenty children to over one hundred and financed partly by local organisations and partly by the central Basque children's fund. Certain of the homes were completely self-sufficient but others became a significant drain on the Committee's central resources.

A listing of the homes showing the amounts paid out from the centre up to 31 August 1937 gives a good idea of the scale of the undertaking on which these philanthropists had embarked. The list shows thirty-four homes for which a total of just over £3,400 had been paid out. The amounts paid out to the homes varied enormously. Camberley, which had sixty children, had already received over £630, of which £215 was for equipment whereas Margate, with seventy-five children in its care, had received only £217.

Charges varied, depending on the physical condition of the houses that were used, the amount of equipment needed to furnish the home and provide adequate recreation for the children and on the extent to which the local committee was able to raise funds for the maintenance of the children. The drive to obtain private sponsorship of children through 'adoptions' at ten shillings per head per week (the average cost of maintenance) began very early on as a means of reducing pressure on funds. By the end of August, nearly 290 children in various homes were being paid for in this way. Salaries of staff were normally paid by the local committees.

Inevitably, some homes ran into financial difficulties. By September, the Worthing home, which had sixty children in its care, was substantially in debt and asked the central Committee if it could not guarantee an overdraft with the bank. In Wilfrid Roberts's estimation, 'it would be a very bad precedent to allow centres to run up debts and then to come to us to guarantee the overdraft.' In theory, he was absolutely right to try and stem the flow of bad debts before they became unmanageable and he took a hard line initially with the Worthing home, agreeing only to a weekly payment of £19-10-00 which was to be reviewed after a fortnight. On September 8, however, 'Miss Thornycroft telephoned in great distress about money as she has none in the Bank to meet the bills and cannot get an overdraft. Funds are coming in very slowly.' Eventually, Roberts agreed to the Committee's paying off the debts and to help with ideas for fund-raising. He refused to guarantee the overdraft.

Other homes also made requests for exceptional payments, sometimes very large payments, as in the case of the Scarborough home, which requested £500. 'I want it made perfectly clear that I am not prepared to pay out large cheques without knowing what the amounts are for', wrote Wilfrid Roberts in some exasperation.

He was, however, quite willing to pay amounts that had been agreed beforehand or were necessary to maintain harmonious relations with other charitable organisations. A notable case was that of the Christian Volunteer Force which ran a home in Glasgow. Although the understanding of the secretaries in London was that the agreement was for the Basque Children's Committee to pay only maintenance for sixty children in the home, the Christian Volunteer Force sent in a bill for equipment amounting to £79-15-00. A comparison of costs for the same equipment from other sources came to £21-10-4. Roberts pointed out that it would be fairer to compare the costs of new beds rather than old ones. He signed the cheque for the lower amount but was prepared to accept that further payment might prove necessary, in the interests of public relations if no other.

It was estimated in late 1937 that the Committee would have outgoings of at least £500 per week for the foreseeable future and that the financial situation was such that 'an appeal must be made'. Certainly, the costs to date had halved the Committee's bank balance in only two months, from over £10,000 in August to £5,500 in October, while donations, after a tremendous surge in July of nearly £7,000 had dropped down to barely £1,000 per month.

In 1938, the expenditure of the Basque Children's Committee exceeded its incoming funds by £3,000 and the National Joint Committee had to transfer several important sums from its general account to the Basque Children's Committee. The Basque children fairly quickly became the 'greatest drain on resources', which was at least partially resented by those on the National Joint Committee whose greater interest lay in the relief work in Spain.

In order to assist the local committees in their fund-raising efforts and to co-ordinate any national campaigns, an Organising Sub-Committee was set up in London. Originally, Wilfrid Roberts had envisaged that the hapless Henry Brinton would co-ordinate fund-raising efforts centrally and visit individual homes to advise them on various ways and means of stimulating local contributions. Brinton does not appear to have been much more successful at this than he had been in setting up Stoneham Camp; his bent was more towards the grand gesture than the boring detail required for such an administrative task. The setting up of a special committee helped spread the load of responsibility and to generate ideas.

Various forms of fund-raising were tried or proposed. Some methods, such as sponsoring a 'Mile of Pennies' and '1/- a month' or 'Penny a Week' collections now have a slightly old-fashioned air about them, though 'Penny a Week' collections for good causes were still the vogue in schools up to the sixties. Collecting envelopes were another standard way of raising money and these were produced centrally by the committee who then sold them to the local centres for less than cost at 25/- per ten thousand or 3/- the thousand. Flag days, jumble sales and garden fêtes were all used regularly to boost funds.

A professional fund-raiser, Captain Stavert, organised an appeal in summer 1938 whereby he drafted a pamphlet and letter, to be signed by the Duchess of Atholl, and undertook distribution to 15,000 names. For this his expenses were £206 and he took 10 per cent commission on any takings. The relatively high costs of this venture deterred the committee from taking up Captain Stavert's offer of organising a second appeal some months later. However, by 1939 he had launched another appeal and the funds raised by the 'Stavert Appeal' passed the £1,000 mark.

Advertising in newspapers proved of dubious value. The committee took out an advertisement in the *News Chronicle* in October 1938. It cost £48 and produced £50 in cash, two adoptions and a number of enquiries from other national newspapers. At a committee meeting it was noted that, 'Unfortunately, the advertisement appeared the same day as the News Chronicle appeal for the Czechs.' East European refugees were by then the hot issue and the needs of Basque children were tending to come a poor second in the public eye. It was agreed that, in general, newspaper advertising was not a paying proposition.

Other plans for raising money were rather more ambitious and centred on artists and performers known to be sympathetic to the Republican cause in particular. In this context, the committee benefited from the connections of its members in fashionable or society circles.

Negotiations with the Basque Ballet troupe were unsuccessful as were attempts to find an orchestra for Toscanini, who was known to be sympathetic towards any anti-fascist movement, to give a concert in aid of the children. Pablo Casals, however, offered to delay an American tour to give concerts for Spanish Relief, provided the committee could guarantee at least one very good concert with an imposing list of patrons.

This emphasis on finding VIPs to sponsor or attend concerts and other fund-raising activities was a common thread in all the deliberations concerning raising money. Whereas, nowadays, VIPs might include the likes of film and TV stars or sporting personalities, then the aristocracy were in great demand as were eminent literary or scientific figures. The suggestion was put forward that, since Professor Freud had signed an appeal for the Basque children very willingly, he could be asked to give a lecture in their aid. At the time, the committee had on offer the Ballroom of the American Women's Club, which, it was felt, would be an appropriate venue. Unfortunately, Freud replied that ill-health prevented him from engaging in public speaking.

The children in the various homes also worked hard to raise money. They hand-embroidered dresses, made costumes for dolls, posed for postcards and designed calendars. One boy of exceptional artistic ability, Jose Alberdi, designed a Christmas card for which an order of two thousand was placed by just one man. Alberdi later became a well-known sculptor whose public commissions included *Nameless abstract* in the centre of Stevenage and *Alma Mater* in the back quadrangle of Exeter College, Oxford. More importantly, by far the largest contribution to funds from a single source was due almost entirely to the children's own efforts.

As early as July 1937, the Basque Children's Committee took note that requests had been coming into the office for the children to give local concerts to help committees in different parts of the country to raise funds. The Committee approved the idea in principle and at that time Neville Towne, who was still the Entertainments Officer, was supposed to be visiting the homes with a view to advising them on the setting up of such concerts. From these small beginnings evolved a whole series of concerts, both small local ones and major concerts organised by the central office. Frida Stewart was appointed early on to organise the concerts while two Spanish singers and dancers, the Señoritas Carmona and Bal, travelled to various homes to give advice and instruction at a fee of £1 each per weekend plus expenses.

The appeal of concerts given by the Basque children was obvious. Firstly, people were giving money to be entertained rather than in abstraction for charity. The emotional appeal of these young children, singing and dancing their local dances and dressed in costume was strong. Since the children made their own costumes and, as performers, cost nothing, the concerts were relatively inexpensive to stage. The publicity generated by concerts had the additional benefit of bringing to people's attention the other ways in which they could help, notably through the 'adoption' scheme.

Fig 6. A Basque children's troupe of dancers in costume. (Private collection)

Receipts from concerts were highly variable, depending on the wealth of the area visited and the size of the halls used. The first major Basque Children's Concert held in April 1938 realised profits of £53, prompting the Basque Children's Committee to comment that 'this was a most satisfactory way of raising money.' Details of various smaller concerts held in 1939 show that one in Fulham raised £8-1-0, another at Birmingham £27 and others held as far apart as Cheltenham and Caerleon anything between £8 and £20. The extent to which concerts were used for money-raising can be estimated by the fact that between 7 January and 16 June, 1939 more than £395 had been raised by concerts in Britain.

So dependent did the committees become on concerts that when, for example, the Yorkshire Committee pointed out that it was having difficulties raising funds, the immediate response was to send up Frida Stewart to discuss the possibilities for further concerts in the area. In Leslie Dow's view (he was an active member of the committee in Ipswich), 'all campaigns, national or local, should be initiated by series of concerts'. Whenever the Committee was running low on funds, the answer was seen to lie in more concert tours. Certainly, they were effective - a series of tours held in the summer of 1938 raised over £750.

The Programme for a tour made by one group of children in September of that year indicates the work that was required and the demands such tours must have made on the children involved. Starting on 1 September and finishing 14 September, the tour took in ten different towns and fourteen concerts. Each concert had 20 different songs and dances with a suitably English finale when the children sang Daisy, Daisy, Two Lovely Black Eyes and Tipperary - an artful conceit designed to wring the maximum emotional response from the audiences. The report on the concerts noted that the audiences had been particularly taken with the performance of the youngest member of the troupe, Juanita, who was only eight years old. Given the intensity of the concert schedules and the amount of work required to stage them, it's a wonder that the children involved found time for any other form of recreation or indeed studies.

Concern was expressed from time to time over the effect that the concerts might be having on the children. In June 1938, Frida Stewart proposed taking a small troupe of four boys and one man on a tour using a Youth Foodship Lorry and Miss Kathleen McColgan suggested that a group of eight could usefully make a tour of Northern Ireland. The Committee thought such a scheme could be adopted 'provided that the welfare of the children was not affected.' The author of a paper discussing the possibilities of four major tours as well as the potential benefits of an American tour remarked, 'I do not think these concerts tire the children or are bad for them in any way. They thoroughly enjoy dancing and singing and are not in the least self-conscious or spoilt by admiring voices.' J MacCallum Scott, then Acting Secretary of the Organising Committee, took a different view, 'Isolated concerts - one in every few months - cannot do any harm. But a continual round of concerts must surely have an adverse effect on the children.'

Dr Betty Morgan, when drawing up plans for the Winter Campaign of the same year, expressed the pious hope that 'this Winter we want the Basque children to be disturbed as little as possible in their studies, but Basque Children's Concerts in secondary and public schools would be worth attempting and could lead (apart from other desirable results) to adoptions.' This concern with the children's education could be compared with the somewhat grudging decision in October 'that £2 might be spent on exercise books for the children if it proved impossible to secure any as gifts.' In reality, the success of the concerts was too great an attraction for Committee members to be unduly worried about the effect they might be having on the children.

A concert tour of the winter sports resorts in Switzerland, involving a group from the Middlesbrough home, resulted in proceeds, after expenses, of over £250. The Middlesbrough troupe was one of the three or four quasi-professional troupes from the homes that raised significant sums of money for the central funds. This was in spite of the fact that by February 1939 the home itself had run up debts of more than £245 and had a bank balance of only £56. Since the total profits of the troupe's tours had been paid in centrally, it was recognised that 'the Middlesbrough home had some claim on the Central Committee', and efforts were made to help them in their financial difficulties.

It might be assumed that the proceeds from the children's tours would automatically have been used only for the children themselves. This became less and less the case as other forms of fund-raising diminished in importance and the demands on the National Joint Committee and other bodies concerned with Spanish Relief and the care of adult Spanish refugees increased significantly. The Winter Campaign plan included one or two large concerts, to be sponsored if possible by national newspapers, solely to raise money for work in Eastern Spain. The £120 raised from a tour in April 1939 was split evenly between the children and the (adult) Refugee Fund. Again, in June of the same year, Frida Stewart was arranging a series of thirteen concerts in collaboration with local Spanish Relief committees - the proceeds to be equally divided between the children and adult refugees.

The problems encountered in raising funds for relief work were such that it was proposed that the children could also perform at Aid Spain and Foodship meetings, particularly Children's Foodship Campaign meetings. This too was agreed to, provided that a statement was made from the platform that the children were not concerned with politics but with relief; a fine distinction given the left-wing bias of such meetings.

As the homes were so dependent on their performing children, they were concerned at the possible repatriation of their stars or loss of their services through some other reason. An outstanding contributor was a musician, Joseba Badiola, who played the txistu (a Basque fipple flute) very well and asked that he be sent a Basque drum by his father, then in a camp in France. The cost was £1. The Committee agreed to this since he was so invaluable in the training of the Camberley troupe. Moreover, because of the need for his services he had not been allowed to take up a position in London that he had wanted. The Committee decided to appeal to other homes to use Badiola's services and agreed to pay him 3/- a week pocket money. Within five months, however, he was sent to France to rejoin his family and a replacement, Fermin Arriba, was found.

In March 1939, Vincent Tewson asked if the Committee could defer the repatriation of children from the Barnet home who were committed to certain concerts. In this case, the Committee stuck to the letter of their repatriation rules but pointed out that the repatriation next planned would not take place till April which should allow time for the children to meet their concert commitments. Ultimately, their repatriation was, in fact, deferred until a second batch of children were sent out.

Over time, the repatriation of some children and closures of under-utilised homes created problems for the concert organisers. In June, Frida Stewart launched an appeal to find out which homes had talented performers or could accommodate the performers from the Bray Court home, which was closing. At about the same time, Miss Morris, the Honorary Secretary of the Yorkshire Council for Spanish Refugees, queried the decision to close the Keighley home on the grounds that it had raised a thousand pounds through its concert work. Clearly, in some people's minds, at least, fund-raising through the concerts had become almost an end in itself.

The involvement of Frida Stewart in the concerts produced a useful spin-off in the form of a Basque children's song book, which she produced in collaboration with John Goss. The costs of production were sixpence per copy and the sales price two shillings. James Boswell, the well-known illustrator, provided some charming pen and ink drawings for the book, which had a foreword by the Duchess of Atholl. *Songs of the Basque Children* made steady sales throughout 1938 and 1939, but the overall contribution to the Basque Children's funds was small, perhaps less than £100.

More money came in through the sales of the National Joint Committee's Spanish Relief Bulletin. At one stage it had been thought to produce a bulletin exclusively concerned with the Basque children, but the response, in terms of suitable articles, was too small to justify a separate publication. The Bulletin was a powerful instrument. Although it cost only 1d to buy, it also brought in substantial sums from the appeals it printed. The October 1938 Bulletin brought in £1,100, of which £275 was earmarked for the children.

AUNQUE ME VES
(BASQUE JOTA)

BASQUE DANCE-SONG

Mud on my feet and clogs I bear,
But I've not been minding the cattle, dear,
I've just been dancing up and down
With the best of all the lads in the town.
Here's good luck to you, and to Jacky too,
For he's happy and knows how good beer to brew.

Fig 7. Page from Songs of the Basque Children, published for The Basque Children's Committee by PEOPLE'S SONGS DISTRIBUTORS.

The October Bulletin, Number 16 in the series, was an interesting one since it gave a lot of information on the Basque children's activities and also set out the aims of the National Joint Committee's Winter Campaign. News of concerts abounds. According to the Bulletin, a tour of Northern Ireland, under the patronage of the Earl and Countess of Antrim and the Marchioness of Donegal was a particular success: 'Joseba Badiola, the chistu (txistu was obviously thought too strange a word) and tambor player, was an outstanding success, due partly to his very considerable musical ability, and partly to the fact that his chistu resembled so closely the Ould Orange Flute! Manolo Esnarrizaga became famous as 'The Boy with the Golden Voice' and achieved fame off-stage by his varied and hair-raising escapades in the Belfast Zoo.'

The tone of all the entries was similarly up-beat, a determined optimism and careful praise of local volunteer groups in their efforts at fund-raising were the order of the day. The slogan for the Basque Children's Committee was declared to be 'Every Basque Children's Home self-supporting, and 500 fresh adoptions by Christmas!' With 1,700 children still in their care in over forty homes, the slogan certainly represented the central committee's concern to boost funds as well as to take some of the pressure off the National Joint Committee's finances. The reasoning was clearly expressed in the National Joint Committee's own aims for its Winter Campaign which were:

'1. To raise £1,000 a week for Spanish Relief
2. To place every Basque Children's Home on a sound financial basis, so that essential funds can be released for relief in Spain itself.'

A sound financial basis was, in effect, one whereby the maximum number of children were adopted, thus removing their maintenance costs from the charges to be borne by either the local or the central committee. Some homes that had proved problematic in the past, such as Margate and Camberley, were able to report that they were nearly self-supporting by April 1939 but overall the finances of the Basque Children's fund were increasingly parlous. By mid-1939 the account was £65 overdrawn and the National Joint Committee had to transfer nearly one thousand pounds during that year from its general account to keep the fund going. Efforts were made, however, to place children in private homes and by April some eighty children had been so placed; their numbers increased as the months went by and homes closed.

Several of the older boys were by this time being looked after under the aegis of a separate fund, the 'London Fund Sub-Committee', dealing with boys old enough to work. Initially, most of these boys were quartered in private homes, the remainder in a Youth Hostel. More suitable accommodation was found, however, at Comeragh Road in West Kensington, into which twelve boys were moved. Another house, in Hampstead, was also used despite the objections of one member of the Administrative Sub-Committee who thought it 'quite unsuitable for the boys as it was filled with very beautiful and valuable furniture and there was no place for the boys to sit in the evenings except in the kitchen or in Miss Burke's living room'. This problem was resolved by moving Miss Burke upstairs (Miss Burke had been in charge of another home before being brought to London to look after the boys).

Little by little the need for a central financial organisation disappeared as more children were repatriated or found private hospitality. The costs of repatriation were not negligible, however, as testified by the allocation of £2,500 from the National Joint Committee's account to the Basque Children's Committee in April 1939 solely for this purpose. In 1938, of the funds that came in to the National Joint Committee, only three shillings were specifically earmarked for repatriation purposes whereas the costs incurred in that year by repatriation came to over £3,700. It is evident that in that year large sums of money that had been contributed by the public for relief work in Eastern Spain were in fact used for various expenses concerned with the Basque children. It is not surprising that those whose real interests lay in the conflict in Spain grew somewhat impatient of the drain on resources represented by the children, living in relative comfort, in Britain.

Chapter Eleven

Repatriation and Internal Disagreement

'Until the parents wish to take them back under conditions of safety we feel it our duty to continue to offer them refuge.'

(Appeal Leaflet of the Basque Children's Committee)

The decision taken at the Joint Meeting of the National Joint Committee and the Basque Children's Committee on 28 October 1937, namely to accept the findings of the Legal Commission concerning which children should be repatriated, was not popular with all the workers in the field. Christopher Hill (the Marxist historian), who was actively involved in one of the homes at Cardiff, was particularly concerned at the possibility that some of the children in his home might be repatriated. Wilfrid Roberts wrote to him on 5 November, taking pains to reassure him that any doubtful cases would be investigated thoroughly and trying to convince him that the findings of the Commission in fact represented a vindication of the Basque Children's Committee policy to date. Politician that he was, Roberts could not resist a small dig at the Communist Party as his passing shot to Hill, 'The breath of criticism of compromising Liberals has reached me. In return I might inform you ......of some criticism I have of incompetent members of your party, who are to be found in key positions in my office in considerable numbers. Your criticism of the office I therefore willingly accept.'

Amongst those whom Roberts considered incompetent at the time were certainly the press department, as is clear from a letter of his a few days earlier to Lord Allen of Hurstwood, who had agreed to speak at a showing of a film on the Basque children. In it he points out that the publication of the results of the Legal Commission's findings had given rise to a widespread belief that all the children would be going back to Spain in the very near future, which was clearly not the case. That such a misconception could gain ground was laid firmly at the door of those responsible for relations with the press. Roberts outlined some themes for Lord Allen, stressing in particular the need for funds as repatriation of the children was likely to take many months to complete.

Early in 1938, the Duke of Wellington's Repatriation Committee was renewing calls for the immediate repatriation of the remaining children. A letter to *The Times* from Sir Arnold Wilson provoked much indignation in the Basque Children's Committee's office and outside, as witness a letter from one staunch supporter who suggested that 'A British peer whose Spanish estates are dependent on the goodwill of Franco (ie the Duke of Wellington) might have chosen a more graceful occasion for one of his rare contributions to political life.' Emotion would seem to have got the better of this particular writer, however, since he also went on to talk of those working for the children in Britain as 'the gallant and heavily over-worked band of mostly young and often strongly pro-Franco volunteers'. While the first statement may have been correct, the second was clearly not an accurate description.

The Duke of Wellington's committee was a public irritant and through its representations in the press managed on occasion to hurt the Basque Children's Committee's fund-raising efforts. More worrying, however, was the effect that the repatriation process had on the local volunteers in some homes who saw the sending back of the children as a betrayal of their efforts. An extreme case was that of Frank Pittman who was connected with the Leah Manning home in Theydon Bois.

Pittman, a schoolteacher, strongly attacked the decision to send five children from the home back to Spain but more seriously he attacked the motives of the officials in London. With a wanton disregard for the facts, he wrote to the Secretary of the Leah Manning home that, 'It should be a well-known fact by now that important officials of the Basque Children's Committee behave almost as if they were the agents of Franco, and persistently discourage efforts to raise money and to bring the Children's plight before the eyes of the public.'

Pittman used the fact that the home had been able to raise £40 through just one concert and was boosting the number of adoptions as evidence that homes could run themselves. He suggested that an investigation should be made into the activities of some of the organisers of the main committee. His letter was forwarded for comment to Roberts who replied at great length and in detail, rebutting the charges made and pointing out that the home in question depended on central funds for nearly half its maintenance charges. Clearly, slanders of the kind being put about by Pittman had to be stopped early on to avoid disaffection among the voluntary workers at the homes whose political convictions could, on occasion, cloud their judgment of the realities of the situation.

In actual fact, during much of 1938 there seems to have been a tailing off in enthusiasm for the Basque Children's cause by the members of the main Committees. The National Joint Committee held only a few full meetings in that year and, apart from a reference to the adverse impact of the Duke of Wellington's Committee early on, nearly all of its discussions were confined to the problems surrounding relief work in Eastern Spain. The Basque Children's Committee noted the repatriation parties that set off during the year - 500 in January, a further large group in April. Meetings were held intermittently, the major work being undertaken from September by an Administrative Sub-Committee, the activities of which are discussed in more detail later on. A report on conditions in Spain from a Mr Ewald was made to the main Committee in November. Political persecution was dying down: 'One did not hear of very many people being arrested for political opinions now; they had learnt not to express their opinions.' The report concluded that many more children could appropriately be repatriated but investigation on the spot was required. It was agreed to try and secure the services of Dr Byloff of the Save the Children International Union.

Before this decision was taken, however, two internal reports had been written on the question of repatriation, one in July and the other in September, which tell us a great deal about how the question of repatriation was being approached and about the difficulties which were being encountered in trying to run the homes and the committees on an efficient basis. The tone of both reports is remarkably similar, basically one of exasperation with the attitudes towards repatriation that were being shown and one of determined realism, a 'let's face facts' approach whereby both authors endeavoured to be as non-partisan in their approach as possible.

The July report was written by Geoffrey Garratt, an outspoken man at the best of times who had had considerable first-hand experience of conditions in Spain, having been very closely involved with the relief work there. The occasion of his submitting the report was the decision to appoint a new Secretary, following the resignation of Betty Arne. From the outset, Garratt urged that any man [sic] appointed should be fully apprised of the likely short-term nature of any appointment and of the true financial position of the Committee, 'One wants to be very careful to avoid the possibility of a claim for wrongful dismissal.' In his view, the new Secretary should visit all the homes, be given power to act and work within a clearly defined policy.

In Garratt's view there were a number of children still in England who would have been returned to Spain if they had been in different homes. Additionally, he thought that at least some of the homes were bad for the children either through poor physical care or because the lifestyle that the children were leading was an unsuitable preparation for the life they would have to lead on their return.

Garratt had made a rough estimate of the location of the parents of the children then still in Britain. This showed that about a thousand children had one or both parents in Catalonia, 600 had both parents in Western Spain and about 100 in France or Belgium, the remaining hundred's parents were thought to be in Bilbao but enquiry was needed. The argument against sending children to rejoin one parent in Western Spain when the other was in Catalonia did not cut a great deal of ice with Garratt; he did not see why small girls should not return to their mothers even if their fathers were away. The policy on repatriation had to be reappraised in the light of three major considerations: the war was likely to continue for quite some time yet, a Government victory was unlikely and the conditions in Bilbao were fairly satisfactory.

Garratt pointed out that some children were being kept only because their parents were poor or 'for some comparatively unimportant reason such as that they are acting as a link with other children in Russia'. In Garratt's view any reappraisal ought to leave only two categories of children, those who definitely could not rejoin their parents and those about whose parents no information was available. In the case of the second category, Garratt foresaw that they might at a later stage have to be entrusted to some official body, perhaps 'some Spanish Government'.

Of great concern was the fact that a new appeal would have to be launched in the autumn and Garratt was not optimistic about the results. 'My experience in approaching wealthy people of Left-Wing views for guarantees was very disappointing. They were prepared to put up small sums but very few to guarantee sums of £100 or more.' The question of funds was an important one since the two-month delay in sending back children originally intended for repatriation in March had cost some £2,500.

Garratt urged that a General Meeting be called to enforce some drastic policy changes, 'so that at any rate the retention of children in this country will not depend on the whim of a particular individual in charge of the local home.'

Although Garratt did not obtain the drastic change in policy that he hoped for, a letter was sent to all the homes urging them to repatriate all the children who qualified according to the policy of the Basque Children's Committee. The letter pointed out that boys over fifteen and girls over sixteen could choose but that in principle all children whose parents or parent were in Bilbao and free to receive them should be repatriated. Children who were orphans, or whose parents were in prison, with the Republican forces or political refugees would not be repatriated.

The ultimate responsibility of the two central committees was emphasised as was the fact that funds had been subscribed on the basis of the policy adopted. Additionally, the letter highlighted the need for funds for relief in Eastern Spain - in the preceding months the National Joint Committee had been able to send out only a few consignments of goods worth a few hundred pounds whereas keeping the Basque children was costing £300 per week. It was pointed out that, if the financial position continued to deteriorate, children might have to be returned beyond the remit of the agreed policy.

Finally, the letter appealed to the homes' sense of morality. The abnormal conditions of institutional life might harm the long-term happiness of the children, 'May this not tend to alienate them from their families and make their ultimate return more difficult and painful?' Even if the children could stay permanently, 'would not this be at the expense of other refugees whose need is greater, since the number of refugees allowed to find work in this country is limited by the Government and by public opinion?'

That Garratt's views had little immediate impact is clear, however, from the second of the reports produced in mid-September by JH MacCallum Scott who had been appointed Acting Secretary of the Basque Children's Committee. In anticipation of his leaving his post in October, MacCallum Scott drew up his thoughts on the repatriation issue, which he hoped might form a basis for discussion in committee. Like Garratt he favoured the repatriation of a much larger number of children.

Unlike Garratt, he was much less concerned with the financial question, believing that, if it proved necessary, the money could always be raised. His arguments against keeping the children in Britain centred on the unsuitableness of their lifestyle and the so far unsurmounted difficulties of running the homes on an efficient basis. In MacCallum Scott's view, 'frequently the homes are little better than impromptu camps with the difference that they are under a roof instead of being under canvas' and often provided only inadequate schooling and poor organisation. Conversely, the constant rounds of concerts and the fêting of children in private homes clearly could be doing the children no good when many would have to return, sooner or later, to lives of extreme poverty. He was concerned that the children would 'go soft' and, in answer to those who would argue that the children should enjoy their relatively privileged position as long as possible, he stated bluntly, 'if luxuries are to be provided for children, I do feel that we have enough necessitous cases in this country to deal with before the Spanish children'.

The loss of identity of children brought up for too long in an English way of life combined with, in some homes, overt political indoctrination against anything Fascist would, he was sure, cause tremendous problems for the children and for their families when eventually they did return to their native land. Further, the older boys without work or with inadequate employment were growing demoralised and increasingly difficult to handle.

On top of all this, MacCallum Scott pointed out that the heavy reliance on (self-opinionated) volunteers and the prohibitive cost of putting the homes on anything like a regular basis, such as enjoyed by the Barnardo's homes or the Waifs and Strays organisation, meant that it was unlikely that a smooth-running, self-governing system could ever be created.

In consequence, the Acting Secretary suggested that the categories of children to be repatriated be widened to include all children with one parent in Bilbao, children who were orphans and had no known legal guardian and those over the age of fifteen who ought to be working. He was, however, against returning children who had both parents in Government territory (basically Eastern Spain) or who had one parent dead or missing and the other in Government territory.

Recognising the objections likely to be raised against such a radical change in policy, MacCallum Scott dismissed the potential opposition of the Basque Government which was 'now little better than a legal fiction' and appeared to welcome the possibility that such a change might lead to resignations from the Committee since these 'might enable the Committee to carry on its work more satisfactorily'. The objections of parents separated from their children were outweighed, he thought, by the fact that it was 'better for the children to be with one parent rather than to be in England with no parents at all'. Military conscription was unlikely but hard work in the Labour Corps might do the older boys some good. The danger that the children might be used as hostages would have to be looked into very carefully but the fear of political persecution of parents who had sent their children to England was not seen as sufficient cause for keeping the children; political persecution was bound to continue even once the war was over, when 'We shall have no option at all but to return all the children to Spain'.

If it was not possible to repatriate the much greater number of children envisaged, MacCallum Scott had one last suggestion. An active Sub-Committee of only two or three people should be set up to meet at least once a week with the objective of taking the homes in hand and forcing them to comply with policy and improve their efficiency. That the Sub-Committee should be small and dedicated was necessary in view of the failure of previous sub-committees to maintain momentum; 'there should be no dilly-dallying involving innumerable proposals and counter-proposals. There has been quite enough of that already.'

Both reports reveal a similar frustration with the lack of real central control over the homes and a conviction that the lives being led by the children were unnatural and an unrealistic preparation for their ultimate return to Spain. Both writers were sure that all the children would have to go back eventually and that 'sooner' would be better for them in the long run than 'later'. Neither report reached the main Committees for discussion.

An Administrative Sub-Committee was, however, set up and met regularly from the autumn of 1938, discussing individual repatriation cases and problems in the homes. Although scarcely the two or three people envisaged by MacCallum Scott (meetings were regularly attended by about ten), this sub-committee went about its work conscientiously and carefully and really took over much of the work initially undertaken by the main meeting of the Basque Children's

Committee. MacCallum Scott's dismissal of the Basque Government as irrelevant proved mistaken; the Spanish Government, clearly not eager to take on responsibility for the troublesome Basque refugees, issued a decree in October appointing the Basque Government as the responsible and legal guardians of all Basque children who had been repatriated. Señor Uranga of the Basque Delegation was accordingly co-opted onto the Administrative Committee.

Chapter Twelve

The Public Debate

'I am beginning to believe that the whole lamentable business was created and developed for political propaganda purposes.'

(Letter from Luis Calvo to *The Times*, 3 September 1937)

Throughout 1937 and 1938, the Basque Children's Committee was particularly concerned about the need to present its case in the press. Contemporary news and letters columns in *The Times* illustrate vividly the level of the debate that raged concerning the pros and cons of keeping the children in England.

Following the bombing of Guernica, the newspaper reflected the general mood of sympathy then felt for the civilian victims of the war in Spain. No fewer than 15 politicians from all sides of the House signed an appeal published on 1 May 1937 for donations for the evacuation of Basque children. An article on 7 May quoted from a letter sent to the National Joint Committee by Archbishop Hinsley, 'We are most anxious to help in this work of saving and of caring for the poor victims of the cruel war. I have a list of our schools where boys and girls could be housed. I am quite sure that our different organisations and societies will gladly help in this good work.' On 8 May, a meeting at the Queen's Hall was reported at which statements were made by, among others, T McEwen, part owner of the *Seven Seas Spray,* the first ship to break the Bilbao blockade, and by the Archbishop of York and Dr Scott Lidgett. The report quoted Isabel

Brown, of Spanish Medical Aid, as saying that the National Joint Committee wanted to 'adopt' 4,000 children.

On 24 May, in common with other newspapers, *The Times* published a number of photographs of the arrival of the Basque Children at Southampton and at the camp. Up to the arrival of the children, the coverage of the story was favourable and dissenting voices were not given a public airing. By July the picture had changed.

In a debate in the House of Lords on 8 July, Lord Newton criticised the presence of the Basque refugee children in the country. In response, the Committee took the opportunity to send a letter from the Duke of Atholl to *The Times*, which published it on 13 July. By this time, other newspapers, especially the Catholic press, had been carrying articles about the call to repatriate the children from such as Sturrup. The Duke was careful to emphasise his own lack of involvement with the Basque Children's Committee, 'I understand that the committee's policy has always been to reunite the children with their parents or those entitled to speak for them at the earliest possible opportunity.'

Raising the question in the correspondence columns of *The Times* was a mixed blessing, as shown by the publication on 17 July of a somewhat double-edged letter from Lieutenant-Colonel P R Butler, 'A cardinal point in favour of the retention of the Basque children in this country is that, in retaining them, we give General Franco and his staff fewer mouths to feed. But, if this fact be realised by some of those who are at present most solicitous for the welfare of these unfortunate little people, they may start chartering their ship again as soon as possible.'

By late July, the problem of the bigger boys' behaviour was being highlighted and articles appeared concerning the imminent departure of 'disorderly boys' back to Spain. Parliamentary Question Time, as reported on 30 July, gave Mr Petherick (Penryn and Falmouth) the opportunity to express concern over the mental condition of the children who had been most troublesome and to seek assurances that the Home Office 'will pay very great attention to the children who remain in other parts of the country to make sure that such disturbances do not recur.'

If the Committees hoped that by sending back the worst offenders the incidents of disruptive behaviour would be forgotten, they were mistaken. On 11 August a lengthy article by a 'Special Correspondent' gave a detailed analysis of the recent troubles, reviewing the arrangements in the homes and pointing out what the author considered to be weaknesses in the handling of the children by their benefactors. Although the writer praised the work of the doctor in charge of medical activities at Stoneham and emphasised the difficulties involved in overseeing a large number of highly disparate homes, the impression given by the article was not favourable.

In particular, the article went into graphic detail concerning the troubles at Brechfa. Sixty boys from the camp, including 'five leading lights' from Scarborough, with nothing to do, gravitated towards the village and held up motorists for cigarettes and pennies. Three drove off in a car, smashed a fisherman's Bentley and stole a lamp. The fisherman complained at the camp and there was a scuffle between a Spanish and a Welsh boy. After dark the boys marched on the village, 'preceded by a camp officer crying to the villagers to bar their windows and remove their cars'. The next day the boys raided an orchard and there was a minor confrontation with the police. The article went on, 'Fifteen boys have left and Señor Hernando, a Spanish professor with an English wife who cleared up Scarborough after the trouble, is now in charge.'

One of the reasons given for the boys' behaviour was the effect of the war conditions in Bilbao: 'Most of them, with a father at the front and a mother standing in food queues for long hours, have been running wild for a year. It should be remembered that the Spanish boy tends to have a swagger and a confidence in his own maturity from two to three years in advance of an English boy of the same age.' The other major reason given was the inadequate discipline in the home including the lack of corporal punishment.

The article ended with a somewhat backhanded compliment to those in charge of the children, 'Now that the wildest boys have gone, one may expect the Basques to disappear from the public eye, unless minor misdemeanours which would be common to children of any race are 'splashed' in the news. Certainly the children are neither as angelic nor as diabolic, as their friends or their critics protest them to be; the trouble seems to have been that their hosts were not as firm and effective as they were generous.' So long and critical an article was clearly most unwelcome to the National Joint Committee and its sister committee.

On 13 August, *The Times* carried an article about a circular produced by the National Joint Committee to combat the bad publicity generated by the disorderly conduct of a few of the children. Five main reasons were put forward to explain the behaviour of this minority. First, 'their naturally excitable nervous systems have been desperately overstrained by the experiences through which they have passed'. A few were even definitely abnormal; the National Joint Committee circular quoted the case of one girl who was so terrified of any kind of machine that she had had to be placed in a mental home. Second, it was difficult to find a sufficient number of Spanish-speaking adults to supervise the children. Third, the Ministry of Labour camps at Brechfa and at Scarborough might have given the boys the impression of being concentration camps. Fourth, boys would be boys and the press had greatly exaggerated events. Finally, there had been too much indiscreet political discussion, partly from the Left but mainly from the Right. The Committee pointed out that they had rescued the children with a view to saving them from 'the psychological and moral, as well as the physical, effects of war'. To what extent such arguments would have swayed the opponents of the children's continued stay in England is debatable.

The controversy died down for a couple of weeks until the publication on 3 September of a letter from Luis Calvo, a fervent Francoist, who vehemently opposed the view that the children might suffer if they were sent back to Spain. A few extracts from his long, polemical letter show clearly how opponents of the evacuation cast doubt on the motives of the committees concerned and distorted the argument by raising such red herrings as whether or not all the children concerned were in fact Basque.

Calvo conceded that the initial idea to evacuate the children had been well-intentioned, 'At the outset the impulse was a noble one which could be put down to the ignorance in which people live in England of the state of order and well-being that rules in General Franco's territory.' Franco had offered a neutral zone but 'their foreign protectors, perhaps moved by a politico-humanitarian complex, sheltered them here, not without the approval of their parents, who knew no more than the English that General Franco and his soldiers also preserved unblemished their love of children and the responsibility of bringing them up.'

Of the children in England, only 400, according to Calvo, came from Bilbao, the rest 'are not Basque'. He went on, 'by what right are they being detained in England when the Spanish Authorities ask for their return to bring them up and correct the pernicious tendencies before and during the civil war in a part of Spain where according to the Communist Minister Jesus Hernandez, 'crimes and looting are allowed'.' He praised the work of the Asistencia Social in looking after children in Franco's Nationalist Spain and concluded, 'I am beginning to believe that the whole lamentable business was created and developed for political propaganda purposes, and that, in very truth, would be something quite different to the generous action of the Duke of Wellington.'

Betty Arne's reply three days later affirmed the non-political nature of the Basque Children's Committee and pointed out that Franco had lost interest in the neutral zone himself, to the point that the children had been bombed while they were boarding the *Habana.* Calvo's reply, published on September 9, was a masterpiece of righteous indignation. Having pointed out that the possibility of a neutral zone was dropped because the Basque authorities considered it to be impracticable, he continued, 'the Roman Catholics in England opposed the bringing of the children here; but, once here, they thought it a Christian duty to help them, especially as out of 4000 some 2800 are 'Godless', give the clenched fist salute, and possess a Spanish - and, I regret to say, English vocabulary which (I say with deep sorrow but direct knowledge) needs speedy eradication by decent education and within Spain.'

Calvo went on, 'I see by the newspapers in Bilbao, San Sebastian, and Santander that the retention in England, France, Scandinavia and Russia of the so-called 'Basque' children has caused such indignation that their parents are trying to arrange for their repatriation by other means.' He concluded, 'It is of course preposterous to pretend that Franco's authorities are putting pressure on the parents to ask for their own offspring.'

Other letters were published supporting Calvo's general thesis that the evacuation of the children was at least in some part motivated by political propaganda considerations but then the question disappeared (at least from *The Times*) until October and the announcement of the Legal Commission under Sir Holman Gregory. Craven's resignation was reported mid-October and the Legal Commission's findings published on 29 October.

The public debate shifted to Parliament in early November, particularly in the Lords where Lord Newton renewed his campaign against the presence of the children in the country. The quality of the debate was not high. Lord Newton quite unjustifiably attacked the Duchess of Atholl's motivation in asking whether the delays in sending the children back were not due, possibly 'to the fact that the Duchess of Atholl - obviously a leader in this movement - had so strong an admiration for the Soviet system that she had come to the conclusion that the family institution was an archaic business which had no use in the present day and was really an impediment to uplift and progress? It was grotesque that a Committee should solemnly sit to decide whether a number of children should go back to their parents.' He also asked, 'whether any babies had been born since the Spanish refugees arrived here. If so would they be entitled to claim British nationality? There was a great predilection on the part of the Spaniards for British nationality.'

Viscount Fitzalan emphasised the opposition of Roman Catholics to the evacuation in the first place while the Earl of Denbigh regarded the evacuation as 'all a part of a specious and cunning piece of propaganda put out by the Red Party in Spain and by their friends in this country to confuse the minds of the British people.' The Earl of Listowel replied appropriately on behalf of the Basque Children's

Committee and the National Joint Committee but the most effective rebuttal came from the Earl of Munster who pointed out that it was the National Joint Committee's responsibility to find the best way of returning the children and that the Apostolic Delegate's lists had not been attested to by either the British Ambassador or the British Consul. He concluded, 'the Home Office had no knowledge of any such event as a birth to any of the persons who accompanied the children. If one did occur, apparently, the rumour that Lord Newton would accept the position of the godfather was without foundation.'

In the House of Commons the following day, MPs also expressed their opposition to the evacuation of the children in the first place. Samuel Hoare opined that the sooner the children went back the better and a Croydon MP, H Williams, demanded, 'Will the right honourable gentleman take care in future to prevent the political exploitation of children in this country?'

On 12 November, the repatriation of the first 160 children was reported in *The Times*. On 27 November, a statement on repatriation by Colonel Maurice Alexander KC was given substantial coverage. The colonel reviewed the background to the work of the Legal Commission and emphasised that the Basque Children's Committee's repatriation policy centred on two main concerns - that there should be a minimum of war risk and that the parents should genuinely and individually ask for the return of their children. Colonel Alexander pointed out that he had been supporting about one hundred children on his estate on the Surrey/Hampshire borders since June and that none of these children wanted to return, 'Only the other day each child on my estate was asked personally if he or she would like to go back to Spain. Without a moment's hesitation every child pleaded to be allowed to remain for the present. The children were then asked collectively if any of them desired to be sent back to Spain, and again their unhesitating reply was to beg not to be sent back.'

Any good that might have arisen for the cause of the Basque Children in Britain from the Colonel's contribution was quickly undone with a report on 10 December about troubles at a home in Northumberland. The former Warden, Captain TP Wilson, catalogued a lengthy list of wrongdoing by the children at The Larches in Hexham, five of whom had been sent back to Spain the week before. The boys were said to have stolen knives, attacked the assistant warden with bottles and knives, hacked walls and electric light fittings, set fire to beds, attacked the matron, broken every pane of glass and the crockery, smashed the gas-stove, broken fences and destroyed plants and shrubs. Gordon P Evans, the Secretary of the Newcastle Basque Children Welfare Committee, said that the allegations were greatly exaggerated although he agreed that there had been 'little outbreaks of trouble' and also admitted, 'All the boys are experts with catapults and consequently windows have suffered, but I am sure there has been no malicious damage.' It is not to be wondered at if contributions to the Basque Children's Fund dropped in the wake of such stories.

By 1938, interest in the Basque children became more spasmodic with a flurry of letters in the early months and a resurgence of interest towards the end of the year. Towards the end of January, a letter was published in *The Times* under the signatures of Atholl, Listowel, Rathbone and Tewson. In it, they explained that since the authorities in Bilbao had given permission for a delegation from the Basque Children's Committee to go to Bilbao (ten weeks earlier) over one thousand children had been repatriated, of whom all but 46 had gone to Insurgent Spain. Further applications were being dealt with but it was likely that a large number of children would remain on the Basque Children's Committee's hands for a while to come, 'We earnestly hope that all the misunderstandings that have been caused by the campaign to send the children back to insurgent Spain, irrespective of the wishes of the parents, will not affect the continued support of those generous people who rallied to help the children when we snatched them from the horrors of Bilbao.'

Sir Arnold Wilson of the Spanish Children's Repatriation Committee replied quickly and at some length to this new appeal for help with the Basque Children. The Committee's letter had referred to Father Gabana as an employee of the insurgents and Wilson took them to task for this discourtesy to the Apostolic Delegate's representative. The real purpose of his letter, however, was to emphasise the legitimacy of the campaign being conducted by the Repatriation Committee which, he claimed, 'was formed at the instance of Mgr (now Cardinal) Hinsley because he felt and publicly declared that the National Joint Committee for Spanish Relief had failed to realise its Christian and human responsibility to restore as many children as possible to their families as soon as possible without letting political prejudices interfere'.

In the view of the Repatriation Committee, which counted among its members such stalwart opponents of the children's presence in England as Lord Fitzalan, the National Joint Committee should take up the offer of the Apostolic Delegate 'to receive, and to care for there, all children whose parents, or one of them, have not specifically asked for the retention of their children in England'. Sir Arnold finished his letter by repeating the oft-quoted concern of the Catholic establishment that the children's religious education was suffering from their enforced stay in Britain, 'It should be borne in mind that they are all Catholics and that it is not easy for them to be brought up as such here; some of the literature produced for their benefit is indeed clearly intended to estrange them from the faith of their country.' Sir Arnold produced no evidence, however, to support this claim.

Further letters followed in the next few days from like-minded individuals who reiterated the arguments concerning whether or not the children were really Basque, questioning the difficulties involved in tracing parents and attacking the 'partisan position' of the members of the Basque Children's Committee. Other letters put forward the views of the Basque Children's Committee members. Edith Pye expressed concern at the possibility of sending the children back to face, yet again, the horrors of warfare while the Basque Children's Committee's official reply to the accusations levelled against it pointed out that not all the children were in fact Catholic and that even those who were Catholic largely belonged to families opposed to Franco. Dame Janet Campbell also entered the fray to make clear that following her and Dr Norman White's discussions with parents and the authorities in Bilbao, there was now 'no reason why any parent should be unable to ascertain the whereabouts of a child or to apply for his return'.

The correspondence died down for several months but the end of 1938 was marked by an appeal by the General Relief Fund for Distressed Women and Children in Spain (the relief organisation held in Government circles to be more impartial than the National Joint Committee and itself on relatively poor terms with the National Joint Committee). This appeal was clearly worded to emphasise the very different approach of the General Relief Fund and, indirectly, can be seen as a clear criticism of the evacuation of the Basque children.

Recounting that the Fund carried out work on both the Nationalist side and the Government side of Spain, Lady Chamberlain wrote, 'All this work has been of a non-political and impartial character..... Care has been taken to avoid any step that might be considered as intervention, and our committee is in no way responsible for the separation of children from their parents or their removal from Spanish soil............Unfortunately we are now faced with the prospect of having to suspend our work owing to lack of funds. Of the £13,000 raised so far less than 6 per cent had been required for expenses and of the rest very little remains..............I appeal to all who have the sufferings of humanity at heart, and particularly to those who care for children.....'

While the Basque Children's Committee was being criticised in public by a fellow relief organisation, the image of the Basque Children's cause could not have been helped by the news item which appeared in early December concerning a certain Mrs Alice Theodora Reeve who was sentenced to three months' imprisonment at Birkenhead for obtaining money under false pretences by pretending to collect money on behalf of the Basque Children housed at Upton.

1938 had ended rather badly for the Basque Children's Committee but during the early months of the following year little or no interest was shown in the fate of the remaining Basque children, at least in the columns of *The Times.* The Committee was able to get on quietly with the job of looking after the remaining children, repatriating some and moving others among the dwindling numbers of homes. Quietly, that is, until November when, following a renewed campaign by the Basque Children's Committee for appeals for funds in the press, Arthur

F Loveday, Honorary Secretary of the Spanish Children's Repatriation Committee, wrote at some length and indignation to *The Times*.

In the eyes of the Repatriation Committee, the subject of the children's continuing presence in England was 'no longer a controversial but a national one'. Loveday used the weapons of innuendo to some effect in his opening lines, 'Let us put on one side the old questions; whether it was necessary for the safety of these children to take them from Spain, or whether they were evacuated as left-wing political propaganda; whether they have been improved and educated by their stay in England, or whether they have many of them have been converted in Christ-hating little Communists, as some of their hosts declare.' As usual, the Repatriation Committee gave no evidence to support these claims.

The main thrust of Loveday's letter was that the children should unhesitatingly be sent back to Spain unless their parents wrote and asked for their retention on account of fears for their safety and for no other reason. The social welfare services in Spain were praised as excellent organisations to take over the care of the children and to seek out their parents if necessary. Loveday's parting shot concerned reports of adoption of certain of the children: 'Another warning I would give to those kind people who, according to a London newspaper have 'legally adopted' some of these children. They should investigate and see if they have the legal or moral right to adopt children who are citizens of another country without the written consent of the children's parents or guardians, duly authorised by the Spanish authorities.'

Some ten days after the appearance of Loveday's letter the House of Lords was home to questions from the usual concerned peers about the status of the children and how soon they would be repatriated. Indicative of the rumours that had been spread concerning the children was a reply from Lord Listowel that he wished to clear up one misconception in particular, 'The committee had not received any money at any time from Russia.' The Marquess of Dufferin and Ava, Under Secretary at the Colonial Office, replied on the Government's behalf that of the 4,000 children originally evacuated, 3,000 had already gone back and 500 were to be repatriated shortly. The Government would continue to press on the Spanish Ambassador and Government the need to restore as many children as possible to their parents.

It was not until 27 November that *The Times* published a letter from the Basque Children's Committee rebutting Loveday's critical letter of a fortnight earlier. Signed by Wilfrid Roberts and Eleanor Rathbone, the letter answered the charges made by Loveday concerning such matters as the cost to the country of keeping the children in England - the financial burden was being borne entirely by the committee and its supporters - and the alleged turning away of the children from their Catholic heritage - great care had been taken to avoid alienation of the children from their faith, religious or political. The two MPs emphasised that the great majority of children had been or were about to be returned and that of those who were left, 'some are boys and girls over 15 who are able to maintain themselves in occupations permitted to aliens, and are known to have such strong pro-Republican feelings that it would be cruel and indeed unsafe to force them after two and a half years in free-speaking England to return under present conditions.' The question of adoptions was also addressed, 'Some are orphans who have been adopted in effect though not legally (since the law does not permit legal adoption of aliens) by foster-parents who have vehemently protested against being deprived of children who are as dear to them as their own.'

This was the last major sequence of letters to appear on the question of the Basque children, not surprising given that Britain had been at war with Germany since September 1939 and more important matters than the fate of a few hundred Basque children were occupying the minds of most people. Furthermore, the numbers of children involved were by now relatively small - both because of the large-scale repatriation which had taken place and, as the Committee had pointed out, a fair number of the children were now virtually grown-up, earning their own keep and decreasingly dependent on assistance from the Committee or others.

Loveday's intervention in November had been particularly galling to the Committee since, in August, following correspondence published in *The Manchester Guardian* on the same subject, Roberts had written to him asking that he refrain from raising the old controversy of the children. Loveday had replied on August 31, maintaining that anything he had written to *The Manchester Guardian* was in the interests of truth and the national interest 'to relieve national homes and pockets at this critical time'. Loveday had added a postscript dated September 2, 'I kept this (letter) back in view of the situation and, as the children cannot I presume now be sent back, I am content to let the matter drop. I presume you will let the MG know.' Only two months later, Loveday had once more entered the fray.

Of course, *The Times* was not the only newspaper to cover the Basque Children's story. Early on, the Catholic press had contained a number of articles generally opposed to the evacuation of the children as, indeed, had the Quaker publication, *The Friend.* Even after the bombing of Guernica in April 1937, when there was much talk of evacuating Basque children to England, the Quaker leadership was expressing doubts about the usefulness of taking children out of the country. Cuthbert Wigham declared in a letter that he was 'doubtful of evacuating the Basque children to England' and a letter from Dr Richard Ellis about the evacuation of the children was prefaced by a statement that the Quakers believed the children were best helped in their own country. It is revealing that *The Friend*'s list of special charities which it urged Friends to support at Christmas time in 1937 did not include the Basque children in England.

Naturally enough, the Catholic papers such as *The Universe* publicised the efforts of Mr Sturrup and of the Apostolic Delegate's representative, Father Gabana, to have the children repatriated. On the other hand, not all the Catholic press could be said to have been unfair on the question. A letter from Roberts to Woodruff, the editor of *The Tablet*, in October 1937 makes the point very clearly, 'I am anxious to write and thank you for the fair statement that appeared in the 'Tablet' of October 16th with regard to the Basque children..............My only object in writing to you at the present moment [Canon Craven had just resigned from the committee] in addition to thanking you for the statement, is to say that the position is still somewhat delicate and I am therefore most grateful to you for your careful handling of it.'

The Committee's viewpoint could be reliably expected from other newspapers such as the *Reynolds News*, the organ of the Co-operative movement, as shown by correspondence between Roberts and Sidney Elliott, the Managing Editor, in November 1939. Roberts asked whether the *Reynolds News* could run an article and appeal for funds for Spanish Relief work to help pay both for the Basque children and Spanish refugees who were maintained in a home at Narbonne in France. 'I know of some of the very valuable work you have done in the past for Spain, and I am wondering if I might ask you to help again.' Elliott replied quickly and promised 'to try to give your work some publicity in 'Reynolds''.

In general terms, the press reported on the Basque children when they made news. For the local papers this might mean a report on the concerts given by the children in the neighbourhood. For the national dailies, after the arrival of the children, the items most likely to reach the public were the tales of wrongdoing by the bigger boys or reports on the scenes at the Franco-Spanish border when the first batches of children were repatriated. An example of the way the press distorted the activities of the Basque children was an article which appeared in the Christmas number of the journal, *Britannia & Eve*, which gave a fictitious account of the bad behaviour of Basque children in a private house to which they had been invited. In this instance, the Committee sought legal advice over a libel action but balked at the potential legal costs, which risked nearing around £1,200.

The political implications of the evacuation and the repatriation controversy tended to be raised in the correspondence columns by the likes of the Repatriation Committee. Throughout this time, the publicity department working for the Basque Children's Committee was essentially reactive and it rarely took the initiative in the public debate. When it had theoretical control on a news story, such as the results of the Legal Commission's enquiry, Wilfrid Roberts for one was not impressed with its handling of it.

One of the problems facing the publicists for the Basque Children was, undoubtedly, that the Basque Children's Committee's stance on the repatriation issue was in many ways illogical when looked at from the viewpoint of the original intention of the evacuation, namely to save the children from the horrors of war. Once it was quite clear that Bilbao would be safe, the Committee began to find other good reasons for not sending the children back, some of which were clearly coloured by the political affiliations of its members. While searching for sustainable reasons why the children should not go back, the Committee had also to contend with the malicious half-truths and distortions of facts put forward by the Repatriation Committee and its supporters. As is often the case, it was far easier for the Basque Children's opponents to attack than for their supporters to defend.

Chapter Thirteen

The Bigger Boys

'Their ideals were politics and football.'

(Poppy Vulliamy)

One of the most serious dilemmas facing the Committees in London in the early stages of the children's stay in Britain was the behaviour of some of the bigger boys. The repatriation of some of the most delinquent elements helped to reduce the problem somewhat but it was clear that most of the homes could not handle the disruptive presence of older boys. A solution was found in the shape of Poppy Vulliamy.

Poppy had helped out at Stoneham with press and publicity work, showing round VIPs and dealing with correspondence with the outside world, including the donors of funds. Poppy was thirty-one, a tall, thin and very energetic young woman, fervently believing in the Republican cause and eager to help the children in any way she could. Believing that most members of the Committees had no understanding of the feelings or attitudes of the older boys, she offered to set up a home exclusively for them. The people in London were 'so frightfully relieved at having somewhere they could send the problems to' that once the home was set up, they left Poppy to run it as she wished with no outside interference.

Initially, a camp was set up at Diss in Norfolk. When Poppy went to meet the boys off the train at Diss station and saw fifty-five 'very large and very aggressive' boys alight, she did momentarily wonder whether she was going to be able to cope. Early events were not reassuring. As soon as the boys saw the apple orchards next to the camp, they raided one and stripped it of its fruit. Poppy called them together and told them severely that the Republic would be judged by their actions and they must, therefore, not steal other people's property in this way. There was no further trouble of this kind.

The local vicar was not convinced of the wisdom of letting loose on a small East Anglian village this group of reputedly delinquent boys and the Sunday after their arrival he preached to the congregation that they must have nothing to do with them as they were 'all little Reds'. The villagers had other ideas, however, and the next Sunday afternoon saw all the boys invited to tea in local homes.

According to Poppy, the boys were very popular in the village, if open to temptation from the friendly village girls. Their stay at Diss was not long, however, as they were camped near the river and winter was approaching. One night, when Poppy was away in London for a central Committee meeting, the river broke its banks and the camp was badly flooded. All the children were housed overnight in the village hall and the camp helpers spent the night trying to salvage goods and tents from the mud. The following day, when Poppy was met off the train by her assistants, she ticked them off severely for their unkempt appearance and dirtiness, arguing that she could not expect the boys to keep themselves clean and presentable with such an example before them. Once she had learned the truth of the previous night's events, she felt very humble. She also decided that the boys had to be moved.

A letter to the local Bishop produced the offer of Rollesby Rectory. Although staying at the Rectory cost virtually nothing, it was not very suitable since there was no heating and Poppy decided that her boys could not stay there for long. A Labour peer, Lord Farringdon, had a huge estate, Buscot Park, near Oxford. Poppy wrote to him suggesting that he should share his stately home with the Basque boys. Farringdon invited Poppy to his home, showed her the priceless antique furniture and the Old Masters on the walls and asked her whether she still thought that the boys should come. Of course, was her reply, he should give away all his art treasures to museums so that ordinary people could enjoy them and then he needn't worry about sharing the home with 55 adolescent boys. Lord Farringdon was not prepared to go that far but agreed to let Poppy use two lodges and the grounds, provided she could raise enough money for necessary equipment and to run the home.

While funds were being raised for the move to Buscot Park, the boys left the singularly uncomfortable rectory for Tythrop House where a mixed colony was set up. The boys' stay there was unfortunate, 'There was a lot of trouble with the older boys and the girls. They should never have been sent to a mixed colony.' In Poppy's view, the home was run very badly by a woman who couldn't speak a word of Spanish and relied on an interpreter. This meant that the bias of the interpreter's views coloured the administrator's opinion, 'bad Spanish is better than using an interpreter.'

Since Tythrop House was not Poppy's responsibility she was able to go often to Oxford to raise money for the boys who moved to Buscot Park after only a few months. Although the boys were staying in the grounds of a stately home, the furnishings were by no means luxurious - iron bedsteads, horsehair mattresses, hard backed chairs - but they had a wonderful amount of space in which to play football on which they were fanatically keen, to swim and go canoeing and generally enjoy a fresh-air, healthy existence. The conditions in which they were living were, moreover, far better than those that they had experienced in Bilbao. Some had eaten gulls and rats, so scant had been the food supplies, whilst one had even been in the fighting.

Given this background of deprivation and the harsh reality of war, it was not surprising that some of the boys were difficult to handle. They were also far more experienced than English boys of the same age when it came to the opposite sex; one boy had been taken to a brothel by his father. The interest shown by the older boys in girls was sufficient for Poppy to read to them the findings of paternity suits and the sort of money that might have to be found if they fathered any illegitimate offspring. This had a salutary effect since the boys were horrified at the sums involved, 'Why, you could go to the cinema every night of the week for that kind of money!'

Discipline in the three homes run by Poppy Vulliamy was administered by the boys themselves. In accordance with Poppy's radical views, she believed that being self-governing would teach the boys more about responsibility and decision-making than a traditional approach would have done. Officers were elected at the Diss camp, at Rollesby and at Buscot Park but generally the same people were chosen each time. The Minister of Education was the least popular as the boys were notably reluctant to take lessons seriously, next came the Minister for Hygiene whose major responsibility was to ensure that the latrines were properly looked after. The Minister of Justice was the most popular despite his seemingly invidious position.

At trials for alleged misbehaviour, Poppy acted as the 'prisoner's friend' since she felt that on occasion the punishments meted out could be too severe. 'Children are much harsher than adults.' She recalled one occasion when some boys who had been throwing their bread around at a mealtime were punished by being refused permission to go swimming for a whole week even though the weather was very hot. Since the boys loved to go swimming, she thought this punishment far too severe but changed her mind when it was explained to her how strongly the boys felt about misuse of food because of the terrible hunger that had persisted in Bilbao. This awareness of the relative comfort of their lives was brought home to Poppy when she found one of the boys sleeping on the wooden floor in preference to his bed. He explained that he felt too guilty sleeping in comfort when the people left behind in Spain were suffering such terrible hardship.

Many of the boys were highly political and fervently anti-Franco. Their views can only have been reinforced by the presence of Gomez, the cook, who was an Anarchist and lent his Anarchist newspapers to the boys to read. Gomez was unusual for a worker at the Bigger Boys colony since he was paid a wage, albeit a small one, 'enough for his cigarettes and newspapers'.

Most of Poppy's helpers were volunteers. Her secretary Marian Heatley had been Churchill's secretary during the First World War, since when she had not worked for a living as she was a wealthy woman and could afford to work free for causes which interested her. She was an invaluable support to Poppy, speaking excellent Spanish and possessing administrative and diplomatic qualities not always to the fore in Poppy who tended to be rather blunt and direct with people she considered incompetent or who she felt did not understand the real needs of 'her boys'. Poppy herself was financially comfortable, living on an allowance from her father.

The male volunteers who came to work in the colony were a mixed bag and generally Poppy found that they were rather unreliable. One turned out be a crook who had been keeping back insurance contributions for himself and he was dismissed. Another who had worked in the mines in South Africa was a homosexual who had clearly been attracted to the colony by the presence of such a large number of good-looking young boys. These were able to take care of themselves, however, and used to laugh about him 'trying it on again'. His big advantage was that he knew about football and organised all the boys' games. Eventually, however, he also left, having decided that he wasn't going to get what he wanted out of his work there. The one exception to the rule was Albert who gave up a very profitable job in Southampton, cleaning out the boilers on the liners, to work at the colony. Though not an educated man he was extremely helpful with anything practical, from digging out latrines to fixing mechanical breakdowns of machinery.

Poppy's skeleton staff did not include either a nurse or a teacher. So, if any of the boys fell ill or proved to be of a delicate disposition, he had to be moved elsewhere. This was the case of one boy in particular who was removed from the Bigger Boys colony to stay at the home run by the Peace Pledge Union, which was far more comfortable and able to look after a relatively weak child. In general, however, the health of the boys was very good and certainly they suffered no epidemics of infectious diseases.

The lack of any teaching staff meant that those boys who were under fourteen years of age were sent to the local school. After that age, the boys' education was effectively over, save for one, Emilio, whose further education at art school was paid for by Solly Zuckerman. At Lord Farringdon's estate it became clear that the older boys would have to be employed in some way if they were to keep out of mischief and use their reserves of adolescent energy in a constructive rather than destructive way. Here again, Poppy was able to enlist Lord Farringdon's help and these older boys were duly apprenticed to the workers on the estate.

One boy worked with the gamekeeper, another in the forestry section, another for the head gardener. In the case of one boy, the work found for him was especially appropriate. He had caused the colony some headaches since he had been caught after stealing no fewer than three cars. Poppy realised, however, that the reason why he was stealing the cars was simply that he loved messing about with the engines. So, Lord Farringdon was persuaded to let this boy work with the chauffeur. From then on, there was no further trouble with stolen cars and the boy became sufficiently skilled to carry out repair work on all the cars, including the two Rolls-Royces. The new apprentices were paid the going rate applicable to such workers, ten shillings per week.

The feeling that they were contributing something to the colony was important to the boys. Initially, when the boys had done something contrary to the rules of the house (and presumably not covered by their own self-governing actions), Poppy had asked that they write out lines from the one Spanish language book she had, *La Vida de las Plantas*. It was not long, however, before a deputation of boys came to her, asking that they do something of practical use instead, such as helping with the food or cleaning, rather than the sterile and boring exercise of writing out lines. Poppy noted how sensible and intelligent this was and readily agreed.

If the boys were fully occupied during weekdays with either school or work, the same could not be said for the long winter evenings during which they seem to have had very little to do apart from occasional debates or playing cards. This was not a well-equipped home in terms of books or toys. Poppy gave the boys a small amount of weekly pocket money and it was up to them to decide how they would spend it. So, if they wanted pencils and paper, for example, they had to buy them, she did not provide them. There were no Spanish books and no cultural outings. The colony was not musical and exceptionally for a Basque Children's home the boys did not raise money by giving concerts. A weekly outing to the cinema was the one diversion open to the boys apart from more physical activities outdoors for which the Farringdon estate was wonderfully suited. According to Poppy, 'Their ideals were politics and football.'

Fig 8. Basque boys' team photo. (Private collection)

Organised religion did not play an important part in the life of the colony either. Of the fifty-five boys, only five registered themselves as Catholics. For as long as the boys were the responsibility of the home, they were not allowed either to change their religion or to assume one. Thus, one of the boys who was taken under the wing of the local vicar and wanted to convert to the Church of England was refused permission to do so while other boys who, on learning of the free food and sports available to those who went to Mass, wanted to register themselves as Catholics were also prevented from doing so. In Poppy's view, the Committee had been allowed to bring the children over on the strict understanding that their religion would not be interfered with and this ruling was interpreted strictly and to the letter.

Finances do not appear to have been a great problem. The accommodation was virtually free as were fresh fruit and vegetables. Minimal expenditure on equipment or home comforts of any kind and the widespread use of the well-established 'adoption' scheme meant that the home could run economically and without recourse to the vigorous fund-raising efforts which characterised so many of the other homes.

Before the colony was set up at Buscot Park, a fund-raising committee had been set up in Oxford and on which sat such distinguished individuals as Bertrand Russell and Professor Carritt. These two stayed interested in the boys for a long time afterwards but most of the committee members lost an active part in the colony once the funds had been raised. Unlike other colonies, there was not a local committee permanently looking after the home's interests; the redoubtable Miss Vulliamy preferred to run the show herself and appeal directly to people or companies, such as Tiptree, who supplied jam, or Marks & Spencer, who supplied unsold produce, rather than work through a committee.

The time taken up with fund-raising, administration of the home and sorting out the problems of the older boys in particular meant that the younger boys tended to be left to fend for themselves. Poppy was to learn many years later from Emilio that the younger boys had felt somewhat neglected and starved of plain affection and that she had always seemed more interested in the 'problems' than in the little ones, who needed a hug and a cuddle now and then to reassure them in this strange new environment. Poppy was not very demonstrative and acknowledged later that it is quite possible that the smaller boys were emotionally neglected.

If there was not much physical demonstration of love, Poppy believed, nonetheless, that she understood the boys far better than many of the other Committee members in London and elsewhere. Both she and her sister Chloe knew Spain well and had got to know Spaniards from all walks of life. Most Committee members, with their privileged backgrounds and often a lack of knowledge of Spain, could not really understand the motivation of some of the older Basque children. A case in point was the tutor to Prieto's son (Prieto was a moderate Socialist leader and Minister in the Republican Government) who helped out at Stoneham Camp. This Englishman was, in Poppy's opinion, hopeless because he had only known upper-class children through his work and could not even begin to relate to some of the boys now in his charge.

That the boys who stayed in the colony appreciated what was done for them is manifested in the way a number of them kept up with Poppy even many years after they had left England to return to their families. (Of the 55 boys in the colony, all but eight returned either to Spain or France.) One relied on Poppy's judgment so much that he even sent his girlfriend to England for vetting by her.

After the bigger boys' colony had been running for about a year, Poppy felt that she was no longer really needed there and decided that she would better serve the cause of Spain by going to work in the still-Republican province of Catalonia. An Austrian Jewish refugee, Walter Leonard, whom the two Vulliamy sisters had met in Spain, was appointed to take over the running of the home and Poppy left for Spain. Her active involvement with the Basque children in England now ceased but in Catalonia she was able to devote much of her time to looking after orphaned or homeless boys, running a farm colony for which she begged, borrowed and commandeered equipment and livestock in much the same forthright and energetic ways she had earlier employed for the sake of 'her boys' in England

Chapter Fourteen

Politics

'..the local Labour Party organiser has issued a circular forbidding members from joining a committee on which Communists are represented.'

(Molly Miller to Wilfrid Roberts, September 1937)

A major problem facing the Committee members responsible for the children was to avoid their becoming targets for political propaganda or exploitation by the two opposing sides in the Civil War. The accusations levelled by the likes of the Spanish Children's Repatriation Committee and its supporters that the children were being turned into 'Christ-hating little communists' and the clear distrust of the National Joint Committee's motivation shown by people like Mr Golden of the Save the Children Union made it all the more important that any attempts to spread propaganda in the homes be stamped on as early as possible.

Neville Towne, the first Entertainments Officer, was dismissed at least in part because of his overt political opinions. Eric Pittman, a helper at Stoneham Camp, also ran into trouble for too flagrant a display of his political affiliation (though, in his case, the affiliation was firmly anti-Franco). In a letter to Mrs Jessie Thomas of the Theydon Bois home, Wilfrid Roberts wrote, 'Eric Pittman was an excellent worker, but he was not too popular down at the Camp and he was one of the few people who I was asked to remove from the camp, as he was supposed to be encouraging too energetic a singing of the

International and other activities which were discouraged.'

Overall, however, the instances of helpers having to be removed because of their over-zealous politicisation of the children appear to have been very few.

It is clear, nonetheless, that the majority of people involved in the Committees' work were opposed to the Nationalist side in the Civil War and that quite a few were Communists. This caused problems in terms of co-operation with other political groupings. For example, in September 1937, Molly Miller wrote to Roberts about a delicate situation in Scotland. 'They are having difficulty there as is experienced all over Scotland because the local Labour Party organiser has issued a circular forbidding members from joining a committee on which Communists are represented. I thought of taking it up with Tewson but I am not sure that it would be tactful to do so.'

If the presence of Communists on local committees created administrative problems, attempts to spread propaganda through covert means were a more serious cause of concern. Ronald Thackrah, who was closely involved with the National Joint Committee in the forties, recalled his dealings with *Amistad* (Friendship), a magazine started in 1940 for the 'Spanish Boys in England': 'It soon became evident that this was a communist propaganda sheet, and as it was published under the aegis of the Committee, I was given the invidious task of censoring it.'

The first issue of *Amistad* was published on May 23, 1940, exactly three years after the children's arrival in England. The magazine was published by the Basque Boys Training Committee, of which Molly Garrett was the Secretary, and its tone was set in her forward to readers, which urged donations be sent to help keep the older boys in England, 'if at any time voluntary support is not forthcoming we shall have absolutely no alternative than to return them to Fascist Spain.'

Consisting of articles and sketches by the boys themselves, the first issue was largely an emotional review of the boys' thoughts about the country they had left and the kindness of the English people who had looked after them. The tone of the articles is uncompromisingly anti-Franco and no reader could have been left in doubt about the sympathies of the authors (and, by inference, of the Basque Boys Committee).

Fig 9. The first edition of Amistad.

'When we first came to England we laboured under a number of handicaps, both mental and material. I regret to say that most of our troubles and calamities were due to an infinity of unproven lies about the behaviour of our parents, the cruelty of their acts and their destructive deeds; and the biggest lie of all - or shall I call it 'fear' of the English people - was that Spain had gone communist. Why did they think that? Because Russia sent a few 'planes and war material? All that the Spanish people did was to fight for the right to independence, and for the right to be free.'

This article was signed by Alejandro, aged sixteen.

An article by Jose Antonio, also sixteen, is even stronger in its language and sentiments: '...the conquerors have murdered our fathers, our brothers, and all those who were dear to us. This has been done by the Germans and Italians with the help of four Generals who sold their own homeland......

'The men who have been able to save their lives find themselves in concentration camps or prisons, waiting for a slow death to take possession of them, while their women and children are dying of hunger in the streets or the fields, without finding a hand stretching out to them to give them a piece of bread.........We shall not return to Spain to salute the accomplices in the murder of our fathers and brothers.'

The final entry in the first issue was a quotation from 'Spain under Franco' by A V Phillips, 'Death sentences are passed in Madrid at the rate of a thousand a month.'

Amistad lasted for a number of years but continued to reflect an obsession with the Civil War and the determination of the contributors to live to fight again for freedom in Spain. However, the edition published three years later, for example, was a markedly more polished production than the first with particularly impressive illustrations; an improvement reflected in the increase in selling price from 3d to 6d.

Before the first issue of Amistad appeared, the National Joint Committee had already had trouble with attempts at spreading Communist propaganda among the Spanish refugees living in England. In October 1939, Paul Partos wrote to the National Joint Committee at their offices in South End Road complaining about the appearance of an information sheet that had been sent to many of the Spanish refugees in the country. This 'Boletin de Informacion, Redactado por el Bureau Español de Informacion del Anti-Fascist Relief Committee' was, in Partos's view, clearly intended to give the impression of being an official publication of the 'British Committee for Spanish Relief'.

There was evidence that the Editors of the Boletin had addresses of Spanish refugees, including 'recent changes of address which were only given to your committee'.

Partos was very concerned about the content and tone of the information in the document, which contained, 'behind a superficial mask of objectivity and general anti-fascist attitude an open propaganda on the lines of the Communist party and in favour of Russia.' Partos urged that the British Committee issue a statement of disassociation with the publication, to be circulated to all Spanish refugees on their lists, and that it use its best endeavours to stop the publication of further Bulletins.

Wilfrid Roberts was understandably concerned at the potential damage that a publication such as the Bulletin could do to the Committee's reputation and, more importantly, disturbed at the misuse of information held by the Committee concerning the whereabouts of refugees. He immediately wrote to Pollitt of the British Communist Party, pointing out that he had always been willing to co-operate with all sections of opinion during the course of the Civil War but such co-operation implied that consultations should take place on such questions as propaganda and policy.

He then came to the real point of his letter, 'During the last few months I have, on more than one occasion received reports that members of the Communist Party were making lists and getting information about Spaniards in this country, and, on one occasion in particular, copying lists to be forwarded to London. When I have made enquiries about this I have been assured that it was not correct. I now ask how and where the lists with addresses of Spaniards to whom this bulletin was sent were obtained.

'My only further comment is that the bulletin has created a considerable annoyance amongst certain sections of Spaniards. I do not know if you have any desire to continue to work for Spain in the same way as in the past. I can only say that if you have, those who work with you must have some consideration for others.'

Unfortunately, we do not have Pollitt's reply.

Roberts also wrote to the unknown Editor of the bulletin,

emphasising that the publication had been produced without the authorisation or knowledge of the British Committee for Refugees from Spain and requesting that a statement to that effect be included in the next edition of the bulletin plus a confirmation that the circulation of the bulletin had also been made without the knowledge or approval of the British Committee.

It is worth remembering how concerned Wilfrid Roberts had been in the very early days when the evacuation of the children was first mooted and Leah Manning had requested that help be given to the Russians in chartering a ship for refugees. Association of the Basque Children's cause with Communism had, as far as possible, to be avoided if support was to be maintained among the general British public. It was the Committee's misfortune that the children presented a relatively easy target for Communist propaganda.

While right-wing supporters of Franco railed against the continuing presence of the Basque children in Britain in the press and in Parliament and the far left tried to reach the children through more subtle means, the vast majority of the children themselves were unaware of attempts to politicise their presence in the country. Although it is true that by far the greatest aid for the children came from supporters of the Republican cause in Spain, those still left in Britain cannot remember any instances of politics being preached to them in the homes. They were, however, aware that the helpers in the homes were 'on our side', that is for the Republic and against Franco, and this comforted them.

The charge that the children were being turned into 'Christ-hating little Communists' was unfounded. Many of the older boys arrived in Britain with strongly-held views based on their own experience of the war, the deaths or wounding of their fathers, uncles, cousins and brothers. Valentin, for example, a chauffeur's son, saw two of his friends gunned down in the street by Franco's planes. The clenched fist salutes and outward bravura of these boys may have been represented by those hostile to the children as expressions of an extreme and unwelcome political force but in reality they were the understandably defiant gesture of boys frustrated at being too young to fight for a cause which they had been brought up to believe in more fiercely than can perhaps be imagined today, worried about what might be happening to their families from whom they had been separated and made restless through insufficient activity in their homes.

Originally, the children had been chosen on the basis of the relative strengths of the various political groupings in the Basque country; a system devised to ensure an equitable parcelling out of the safety that would be provided for the children through evacuation. In this sense, the presence of the children was, in spite of themselves, a political question even before they arrived. The political basis of their choosing was reflected in the files kept by the Basque Children's Committee, which recorded the name, date of birth, next of kin in Spain and other essential details of each child on sheets which had two reference numbers (to add to the administrative confusion) - the Bilbao reference number which came off the Asistencia Social's listing and an English reference number which bore no relation whatsoever to the first. Among the details to be recorded were religion but instead of finding the expected Roman Catholic or 'none' we find instead the political affiliation of their family - Socialist, Communist, Basque Nationalist and so on.

Of the children who stayed in Britain through their adulthood, few became actively involved in politics but most maintained a steadfast opposition to Franco, some refusing to return to Spain until the death of the dictator. One expressed whole-hearted support for ETA and welcomed further bloodshed in Spain if it led to a free and independent Euzkadi (Basque Country). This man, surrounded incongruously in a dreary council flat by Euzkadi flags and with a treasured Basque beret carefully laid in one of his dresser drawers, seems to be an isolated case; so too, however, is the son of one of the Basque children's teachers. He became a Conservative MP and Minister - Michael Portillo.

Chapter Fifteen

Life in the Homes

'We had to share chores - cleaning the bathroom, buttering the bread. In the morning we went to school. There were two teachers but one left. Marguerita stayed for five months and then went to Argentina. After that, the lessons stopped'.

(Merche, about the colony at Ipswich)

At one stage, the children were housed in some eighty colonies scattered throughout the country. Homes were set up in Scotland and Wales, in Yorkshire, Lancashire, the North East and North West, Somerset, Leicester, Staffordshire, East Anglia, the South East and London. A preponderance of homes in the North might be explained by the far higher proportion of Catholics in northern Britain - out of the homes in existence in 1938, thirty-two could be found in the counties of Yorkshire, Lancashire, Northumberland and Cumberland.

Scotland was least well represented in terms of homes with only one at Wigton and another at Montrose. The Basque Children's Committee had been keen to increase the number of homes in Scotland but it proved difficult to find suitable accommodation. In early February 1938, the Scottish Co-operative Society suggested a possible home at Rothesay but it needed structural alterations as well as central heating. A friend of the Duchess of Atholl inspected the home and reported adversely on it. The Scottish Coop subsequently decided against using the Rothesay home and opted for 'adopting' children at the Brampton

Home in Cumberland instead.

The Scottish difficulties in finding suitable accommodation were not unusual. Although a number of large country houses were offered to various of the local committees, they often proved to be in such a poor state of repair or to entail such heavy running costs that they could not be used. The policy on whether or not to use a particular building was decided in some cases by the Central Committee, if it was committing funds towards the home, and sometimes by the local organisers. This goes some way to explain the apparent discrepancies in choice of home - Rothesay might have been turned down but a condemned workhouse in Wickham Market, which was filthy, uncomfortable and cold, was used to house the hundred children who first stayed in the gracious Wherstead Park in Ipswich.

The useful life of the homes varied enormously. A camp set up at Dymchurch to take the last couple of hundred children left at Stoneham Camp was opened in mid-September and closed barely a month later when the majority of children had been successfully placed in more permanent homes. By September, two colonies, Barnes and Herstmonceaux, were facing difficulties - the first had to look for new accommodation, the second, comprising only a small number of boys, was shutting down. In December 1937, three homes, those at Thame, Derby and Dorking, were facing imminent closure.

Most dramatic were the problems facing the children who were being looked after by the Salvation Army, which had at an early stage taken on the responsibility for four hundred of the children. Of these, about 350 were housed in one of the Army's centres at Clapton, East London. The Sally Army also ran a home at Hadleigh.

Difficulties were soon encountered at the somewhat crowded Clapton home and, in July, 202 children were removed to a Brixton orphanage. By the end of July, the Salvation Army was asking for the remaining 114 children to be taken from their care completely because the Clapton centre was needed for a conference at the beginning of September. It was reported, moreover, that General Evangeline Booth was not contemplating providing any financial support for these children. The Duchess of Atholl, at a Basque Children's Committee meeting on July 28, observed that the Salvation Army had twice put out a press appeal for funds, stating that it was taking 1,400 children. She was 'sorry that the Salvation Army did not see its way to carrying through (its) earlier promise'. A visit to the indomitable General by Miss Rathbone and Mrs Manning proved unsuccessful.

By November, a letter from Colonel Gordon, the Salvation Army representative on the Basque Children's Committee, stated that the Basque Children's fund was almost exhausted and suggested that the children still in the Army's care be absorbed into the Committee's other homes. Within two months, the Committee had taken over the financial responsibility for the Brixton home while the home at Hadleigh was to be closed down. By April, even the Brixton home was scheduled for closure. The failure of the Salvation Army to keep to its original commitment contrasted sharply with the Catholic Church's contribution, despite the Church's known view that all the children should be repatriated as quickly as possible.

The moving of children from one colony to another was exemplified by Jose's experience. After three or four weeks at Stoneham, he moved to the Salvation Army in Clapton and then to Margate. Within a year, he was on the move again – to Keighley in Yorkshire – and by 1940 he was housed in Arkley and then Margate Laleham. The last colony he stayed in, from 1942 to 1944, was at Woodside Park in London.

As early as mid-July, most of the 1,200 Roman Catholic children had been housed, leaving approximately 150 practising Catholics still at Stoneham Camp. Repatriation reduced the numbers in Catholic homes significantly but there were still five hundred being cared for by the Church at the beginning of 1938. The Church never asked for financial assistance for the children in its care but relations with the Committee were uneasy, following the split caused over the repatriation issue and the resignation of Canon Craven in October 1937.

A major concern of the Committee members was the inadequacy of arrangements for the inspection of the Catholic homes compared with those run by the Committee, which were regularly visited by a small team of inspectors. The Committee was worried by rumours not only of propaganda (in favour of Franco and of repatriation) being disseminated in some of the Catholic homes but also of physical neglect of the children.

Matters came to a head in November 1937 following the death in Newcastle of Angel Renteria, the son of an influential Bilbao family, and a report on the condition of some boys who had been removed from St Dominic's, Ponsbourne, at the request of the Mother Superior. The boys were found to be suffering from scabies, neglect and bad feeding. When the Mother Superior requested that the boys be returned, after she found that the trouble in the home had been caused by English boys and not by the Basques, this was refused because the boys needed to be kept in isolation. Canon Craven was asked if inspections of the Catholic homes could be carried out on a regular basis.

The Canon agreed to medical inspections provided the homes in question also agreed to the proposed visits by the Basque doctor employed by the Committee, Dr Irarragorri. The Newcastle home refused.

Gargle Parade at Bray Court, Maidenhead.

Fig 10. Photo from The Basque Children's Page of a National Joint Committee appeal leaflet, October 1938.

What life was really like in the homes is best told by the children themselves.

Pedro

Pedro came to England when he was twelve, accompanied by a seven-year-old sister. They left behind them two other brothers aged four and fourteen. Their father was a full-time trade-union official in Bilbao who, when the war opened, disappeared for a month, organising the deployment of men and arms to defend Bilbao. After his return he went to fight at the front, where he saw the evacuation scheme advertised in a local newspaper. He wrote to his wife and told her to arrange for the evacuation of the two middle children.

During the war, Pedro's father reached the rank of Brigadier. At the end of the war, he went into hiding in Asturias but after three months decided to give himself up to a certain death. He was sentenced as expected by the authorities but after six months the sentence was commuted to life imprisonment. He was eventually released after eight years.

Meanwhile, the two children had been quickly despatched from Stoneham camp, following their arrival in England, since they were among the four hundred children taken to the Salvation Army hostel at Clapton in East London. Pedro saw his sister only at mealtimes as the boys and girls were segregated from the very beginning. There were no organised activities, a very small play area and, in the eyes of the children, very poor food.

It was not long, however, before the older boys had found a way over the walls and into the streets where the friendly East Enders soon took pity on them and invited them into their homes. Pedro found out about these exciting activities and joined in. He remembered a group of about fifteen boys being caught in a rainstorm and sheltering under a bridge. A door opposite opened and they were all invited inside. Apart from such welcome visits to people's homes, the boys also took advantage of the milk bottles left invitingly outside on the doorsteps. They supplemented their meagre diet further by buying bread from the van that called regularly at the hostel, using money given them through the railings by strangers.

As time went on the boys became more brazen, nipping over the wall in the morning and then sauntering through the main entrance in the evening, when their names were taken down and noted in a book. Pedro frequently sat at the punishment table at mealtimes where supper consisted of two slices of dry bread and a mug of water.

Though well-intentioned, the Salvation Army was ill-equipped to deal with such a large number of boisterous young boys whose temperaments had undoubtedly been affected by their experiences in the war in Spain. Attempts to preach the Gospel fell on deaf ears - the children were herded into the main hall to listen to hymns, the like of which they had not heard before and did not care for, but when some of the children attempted to leave they found that the doors had been locked to keep them inside. Eventually, a coachload of children, including Pedro, was sent back to Stoneham.

Life back at the camp did not interest Pedro, who wanted to go back to his pals and the street adventures in London. Indeed, he was once caught trying to escape from the camp – though he had not worked out how he would make it back to London. New colonies were announced over the loudspeaker system at Stoneham and one day Pedro caught the name of Scarborough. On his journey down to London, he had noticed a poster for the resort depicting the seaside and he decided that that was the place for him and his sister. So, he signed up.

The colony at Scarborough turned out to be several miles from the sea in a collection of Nissen huts, run by a well-meaning Commander Burr, known as the Commandant. For the first three months, this rather makeshift camp served as the Scarborough colony and difficulties abounded. Discipline was extremely difficult to maintain and the camp rapidly gained a poor reputation. The boys broke windows and often escaped to the seaside. One incident in the kitchen turned into a near-riot when a boy, missing a bun from his meal, went to ask for one from the cook who mistakenly thought he was trying to obtain a double helping. As the boy went to take one, the cook inadvertently turned to him with the knife he was holding – the whole camp emptied as the boys chased the cook.

Certain of the older boys were naturally destructive ringleaders. 'I watched two of them systematically break every window in one of the huts,' Pedro recalled. 'They effectively got away with it but I was punished for accidentally breaking one window – I resented that.'

Conditions improved when some of the troublemakers were removed and the rest of the children were moved to an old hospital in Scarborough itself. But Pedro was soon on the move again. He left for Montrose in Scotland in September 1938.

Pedro spoke rather more English than many of the children at Montrose, where the colony had kept very much to itself. Consequently, when local families began to take an interest in the children and wanted to take any of them out, have them to tea or to stay for longer periods, Pedro was often the one to go.

In this way, he met many different people from all classes and backgrounds. 'There was this Polish count who was particularly keen on giving us baths but I worked out that if he tried anything on, apart from scrubbing my back, I could deal with him as I was quite a lot bigger than he was.' At other times, Pedro stayed with a Scottish family on a local housing estate and formed a strong bond with the older son. At the outbreak of World War II, the boy joined up and Pedro refused to go and stay with another local family because 'it would have been disloyal to my friend.'

By December 1939, Pedro had moved to the colony in Barnet, which, in common with many others, could not afford to keep boys of working age, that is those who were fourteen years or older. So, Pedro was sent to work at the local industrial estate in a surgical dressings factory. He did not enjoy the work and set about finding some way to improve both the work and the amount of food he could get hold of. He hit upon working for the local bakery, 'But it was so undignified, delivering bread on a bicycle.' Luckily, a friend helped to find work at a local engineering works, where he stayed throughout the war, making aeroplane parts.

The system operated at Barnet meant that the older children who were working gave the whole of their pay packet to the administration, who returned one shilling in pocket money. From the local committee's viewpoint, this was essential if the home was to keep going but, not unnaturally, the older boys resented losing all their pay. Those on piecework negotiated with the factory to put just the basic pay into the pay-packet and hand over the additional earnings to the boys themselves.

Some of the boys thought the home was badly run and the food poor. 'I and a friend went to the matron to complain and to give some suggestions about how it could improve but she just said. 'If you don't like it, you know what you can do. So, we left.' Pedro was just seventeen at the time.

Juanita

Juanita was born in San Turce, a port near Bilbao. Her father had come from Burgos to work at Los Altos Hornos, the local steel works, and had married a local girl who worked in the fishing industry. He was staunchly pro-Republican and when war was declared he joined up. He died defending the Iron Ring around Bilbao about three months before Juanita and her older sister were evacuated. All the papers had been arranged by their father before his death; their mother did not want her two daughters to be evacuated and was only persuaded to let them go by other members of the family. The girls were aged eight and nine; they left behind their widowed mother and a three-year-old brother.

Juanita and her sister were registered as Catholics and at Stoneham were placed in the Catholic section. Sometimes, children from another part of the camp would come and cut the guy-ropes on the tents and fighting between Catholics and non-Catholics was quite common. Juanita remembered that children were often trying to escape from the camp back to Spain. She and her sister once crawled out of the camp on their hands and knees followed by some twenty other young girls; they were apprehended a couple of miles beyond the perimeter.

Given their religious status, the girls were sent to a convent some two and half months after their arrival. They and about twenty other Basque girls were looked after at the Sisters of Nazareth Convent in Manchester. There were about 100 girls at the school, mainly Irish, as were the nuns. For the first couple of years, the Basques were kept isolated from the rest and mixing was not encouraged. The girls had their own teacher, Joanna de Verastain, 'from quite a high-class Basque family', who gave them their lessons in Spanish. The routine was regimental and highly religious with compulsory Mass at six in the morning. The heavy emphasis on sin and the rigidity of the nuns' outlook turned Juanita against Catholicism, 'When I left the convent, I was very much against religion; my children are not even baptised.'

After the first two years, Joanna de Verastain had to leave the convent to go and teach in a home where there were more Basque children, a number of the girls from the convent having been repatriated. The remaining Basques (by the end there were only six) were plunged straight into the mainstream education of the convent, forbidden to speak Spanish, even among themselves, and drilled hard to make up for lost time so that they could take the public exams at the age of fourteen. Juanita used to cry at being kept in during the afternoon to do extra studying but in the end she grew to love the work and the fact that she could read as much as she wanted. She was proud of her unaccented English.

The convent looked after mainly Irish girls who were orphans or came from large families too poor to support them. It was normal for these children, once they had finished their basic education, to be put to domestic service and sent out to the wealthy Catholic families in the surrounding area, with half their wages going back to the convent. This would have been Juanita's and her sister's future but for the intervention in 1945 of a Dr Duran who had met someone from their stepfather's family (by this time their mother had remarried) who had asked him to look into the welfare of the two girls at the convent. Luckily, Dr Duran lived in Manchester so was able to visit the girls easily. He was very depressed at their situation and fought with the convent authorities for the girls' release. Eventually he won and they went to live with him, his wife and three-year-old son in their three-bedroom flat.

Laureana

Another Basque with first-hand experience of life in the Catholic homes was Laureana. The eldest of five daughters, she had just been given her first teaching post, at the age of twenty, when Guernica was bombed. She was told she could volunteer to accompany a group of children who were being evacuated to England for about three months. She volunteered, 'I was an idealist'. Her four sisters, grandmother and aunt went to France while the parents stayed behind to keep the home going until their return.

When the time came for teachers to leave Stoneham Camp and go to individual homes, 'we were told where to go', and being a devout Catholic, Laureana was sent first to a convent school at Tottington in Lancashire.

There she taught all subjects and also helped to look after the children more generally. The nuns 'welcomed the children with open arms' but made no attempt to conceal their support for Franco and their belief that it was not in the children's best interests to stay in England. Arguments with the nuns, particularly over the depth of Franco's religious sincerity, were fairly common; even pointing out to the nuns the activities of Franco's Moorish troops failed to shake their approval of him. The children at the convent mixed quite freely, according to Laureana, and she felt that the time there was generally a happy one.

Laureana remembered an amusing story concerning a priest who used to visit the teachers. This priest was very kind and used to leave the teachers a few coppers whenever he could. One day, after leaving the convent, he came across a poor Irish labourer who was in a very sad state with broken shoes and very hungry. The priest gave him all the money he had on him. Unfortunately, he had forgotten that he had to buy his return railway ticket to return home. So, the priest went back to Tottington and asked the teachers if he could have back the money he had just given them.

As the financial position of the various homes deteriorated and the central funds also began to ran out, a favourite form of easing the burden was to find local individuals who would be willing to 'adopt' one or more children for ten shillings a week each, the cost of maintenance on average. The kindness of some of these local benefactors went far beyond just paying a sum of money to the local children's home.

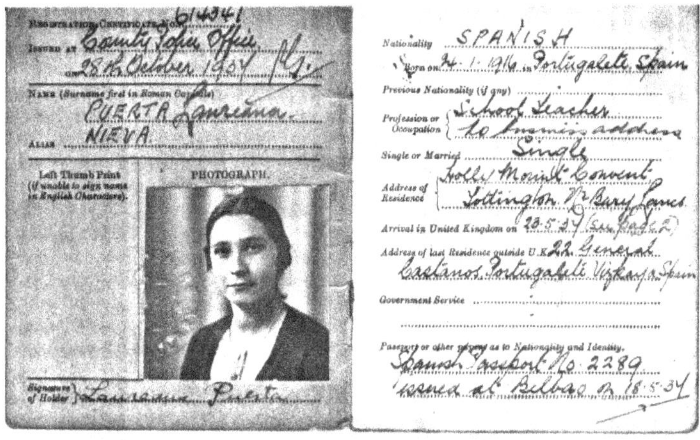

Registration Certificate No. 614341
Issued at County Police Office
on 28th October 1937
Name (Surname first in Roman Capitals) PUERTA Laureana NIEVA
Alias
Left Thumb Print (if unable to sign name in English Characters).
PHOTOGRAPH.
Signature of Holder Laureana Puerta

Nationality SPANISH
Born on 24-1-1916 in Portugalete Spain
Previous Nationality (if any)
Profession or Occupation School Teacher
Single or Married Single
Address of Residence Holly Mount Convent Tottington Nr Bury Lancs
Arrival in United Kingdom on 23-5-37 (see page 2)
Address of last Residence outside U.K. 22 General Castaños Portugalete Vizkaya Spain
Government Service
Passport or other papers as to Nationality and Identity. Spanish Passport No 2289 issued at Bilbao on 18-5-37

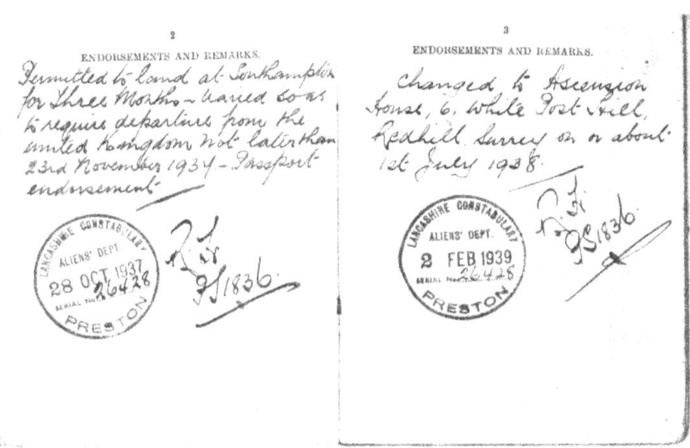

2

ENDORSEMENTS AND REMARKS.

Permitted to land at Southampton for three months – warned so as to require departure from the United Kingdom not later than 23rd November 1937 – Passport endorsement

LANCASHIRE CONSTABULARY ALIENS' DEPT 28 OCT 1937 SERIAL No. 26428 PRESTON

3

ENDORSEMENTS AND REMARKS.

Changed to Ascension House, 6. White Post Hill, Redhill Surrey on or about 1st July 1938

LANCASHIRE CONSTABULARY ALIENS' DEPT 2 FEB 1939 SERIAL No. 26428 PRESTON

Fig 11. Laureana Puerta's British registration card, showing original permission to stay for three months only. (Courtesy Laureana Puerta)

Helvecia

Helvecia's family came from Larboleda, a small village where the father had been a leading Socialist who, together with friends, started the village's first Socialist co-operative. The family was well-known locally and, inevitably, had created enemies among those in the village who secretly supported Franco. Helvecia's father died before the outbreak of the civil war, leaving his widow to cope with the needs of seven children, with the youngest only eight and the eldest in their mid-20s. When the announcement came that families could send their children to England, the decision was to send the three youngest – Helvecia, then fourteen; her brother Elbio, who was ten, and the eight-year-old, Delia.

Elbio, in particular, was very attached to his mother and had been most unwilling to leave her in Spain and go to England. So, he was told that his mother would be joining the three of them shortly. This deception was kept up for several months and it was not unusual to find the small boy standing at the edge of Stoneham camp waiting for his mother to arrive.

Helvecia, as the eldest of the three, assumed the responsibility of choosing the colony they should go to and she chose Carshalton Beeches, a small home comprising groups of children from the same families. They became an extremely close-knit community and, although most went back to Spain after the war, they maintained close contacts with each other, occasionally meeting up for reunions in Spain. Apart from the benefit of living in such a happy home, the children were also lucky to be taken under the wing of George Cadbury, a member of the prominent Quaker family of chocolate fame. That the children's relationship with the Cadburys lasted for the rest of their lives was due in part to an incident at the Carshalton home, which happened some time before they met George Cadbury and his family.

Carshalton Beeches used to receive visits from a man called Peter who, the children there understood, came from the London Committee to enquire after their families in Spain. The Spanish helpers at the home warned Helvecia that Peter's purpose was to find out whether the children had family in Spain who could take them back and advised her not to say that she had heard from her family. Helvecia had, in fact, been receiving letters from Spain and knew that her brother had been wounded in the fighting and that her mother was extremely poor and could not afford to look after her three youngest if they were sent back to her. So Helvecia said that she had heard nothing from her family and had no idea of the whereabouts of her mother. Peter appeared to believe her and no pressure was put on the children to return. (The fact that Helvecia was receiving letters from Spain and the advice given by the Spanish helpers imply at least some collusion on the part of the people running this home to prevent children being repatriated.)

Some time later, the Cadburys decided to 'adopt' a child at the colony, Delia. On hearing that she had a sister, they invited them both to tea. That day also happened to be Elbio's birthday and the Cadburys decided to adopt all three. The children visited the Cadbury home frequently and used to stay there for quite long periods at a time. When news came that Franco had won the war (March 1939), Helvecia was terribly upset at the thought that she, her brother and sister would have to return to Spain. Most of all she was worried that the deception she had kept up about not hearing from her family would have to be revealed and she feared the reaction of their benefactors at having been duped in this way. In awkward English, she explained everything in a long letter and left it for the English family to read. On her return to their home, they showed great understanding and assured her they would do all they could to help the three of them. The Cadburys became their legal guardians.

Valentin

Another Quaker who devoted himself to the cause of the Basque children was Richard West, who was closely involved with the work of the Ascension House colony at Redhill in Surrey. One boy in particular benefited from the care and consideration that Richard West showed towards the young refugees. Valentin's father was one of the chauffeurs to the President of the Basque Republic. His mother was paralysed down the left side and relied greatly on her children for help in the domestic chores. When the decision came whether or not to evacuate any of their children, Valentin's parents decided that only the youngest boy should go, leaving behind the two sisters to help their mother and the oldest boy of fourteen who could go out to work to supplement the family income.

Valentin first stayed at Ascension House after the Park Farm colony at Westcott closed. Ascension House had its own teachers and the children were given daily lessons in Spanish on the basics of learning.

Eventually, however, the children were sent to the local junior school where they did their best to catch up on their education in a foreign language that they spoke only poorly. Valentin stayed at Ascension House until the outbreak of the Second World War, when the children were dispersed and Valentin and his best friend Miguel were sent first for a short while to Bexley Heath and then back to Dorking, to stay in the home of the woman who had acted as cook at Park Farm.

Neither boy felt really at home, rather that they were being looked after because the family was paid to do so and not out of any real feeling for the boys themselves. The two boys went to the local school, St Paul's, returned home for tea and then were sent out of the house to play outside until 8.00 or 8.30 at which time they returned, had their night-cap of cocoa and went to bed. As Valentin put it, 'It was supposed to be a home but we were only fed and watered'. The loneliness of the little boy of eleven can be imagined.

After nine months, the boys returned to Ascension House, which now provided shelter for adult refugees, not just Basques but Austrians and others who had fled from the war raging in Europe. Richard West decided that the boys would be better off with other children and he had them moved to Spurgeon's Orphanage in Reigate. Miguel left the orphanage at the age of fourteen to work in the kitchen of the Duke of Sutherland's estate at Guildford. Valentin was put forward for the entrance examination to Redhill Technical School; he passed and studied electrical engineering for the next two years, travelling each day to the college. He was the first boy from the orphanage to continue his education in this way and set a precedent for other boys to follow in the future.

Throughout this time, Richard West was always available for advice and encouragement and would call in on the young boy from time to time; 'He was there (if I needed him), he was like my father'. After Technical School, Richard West found a job for Valentin as an apprentice engineer at a local corporation and Valentin moved into digs at the age of seventeen.

Alicia

As Valentin had found out, however, not all the people who took in Basque children were as caring as the Wests and Cadburys. One girl who found this out the hard way was Alicia, who came over at the age of twelve with one of her brothers, Jose-Pedro, who was then eleven. Their widowed mother and the youngest child Raoul, who was just four, stayed behind but eventually fled to France until the Second World War when they returned to Spain.

From Stoneham, Alicia and her brother had gone first to the colony at Ipswich run by Chloe Vulliamy, the sister of Poppy who ran the home for bigger boys in Norfolk. The children enjoyed their stay in the beautiful surroundings of an old English country house. The boys played football; there were swimming and long walks and weekly Co-op dances. The Co-operative Society also provided free shoes. Eventually, however, the children had to move to another home, which turned out to be the condemned workhouse at Wickham Market. Conditions here were in sharp contrast to Ipswich. The building was gloomy with seemingly endless stone corridors barred at either end by huge doors. It was very cold and exceedingly dirty.

The daily routine, however, was much as it had been at Ipswich. There was school in the morning (four teachers for 100 children), a break for milk, lessons again and then lunch. Lessons were rather rudimentary with the basics of geography, arithmetic and writing being taught by the Basque teachers. An elderly English lady used to come and try to teach the children some English by holding up picture postcards and asking the children to repeat out loud 'house' or 'boat' or 'Tower of London'. She didn't make much progress as the children played her up most of the time. In the afternoon, the girls might sew or there would be music. The older girls had a rota for daily chores such as buttering all the bread for breakfast or doing the washing-up.

Fig 12. Alicia, middle row third from left, with other children and volunteers at one of Chloe Vulliamy's colonies. (Private collection)

Alicia left Wickham Market after a few months to stay with an English family in Sidcup, Kent. There were three children in the family including a small baby. Alicia was expected to do the fires, look after the baby and do the housework. She slept on a sofa in the parlour. Not surprisingly, the young girl became very depressed and thin. She insisted on returning to the colony, much to Chloe Vulliamy's dismay, but one look at Alicia's condition put any thoughts of anger out of her mind and she merely told the girl to go and find something to eat.

Not long after, Alicia went away again, this time to Westcliff to stay with a Miss Bolton who ran a boarding house. When Alicia arrived, just before Easter, there was only one guest in the house but as the season progressed the house rapidly filled up and Alicia was once again working as a full-time maid. Paid 2/6d a week, she slept in the kitchen on two chairs for a bed. She went back again but the colony had by then been split up - her brother had gone to Margate and there were now fewer than twenty children in a little semi-detached house in Ipswich.

With the outbreak of the world war, the Ipswich colony was disbanded and Alicia stayed for a short while in Wilfrid Roberts's house in Hampstead where a number of Spanish refugees were sheltering. Subsequently, the Misses Pollock and Priestley took Alicia under their wing and she stayed with them in Knightsbridge. They were particularly shocked at the state of Alicia's teeth and sent her to their Harley Street dentist to have them dealt with. They were very kind but it was clear that Alicia could not stay with them indefinitely. Through a friend, Alicia met Julia and Goody North who lived in Maida Vale. The older woman and the young girl took an instant liking to each other and Julia North offered Alicia a home with them, 'I could go and live there - not as a domestic but as one of the family; that sounded rather lovely'.

Domestic service was not an uncommon fate for the Basque girls, once they reached the age of fourteen or thereabouts. Before the outbreak of the war in 1939, it was very difficult to secure more satisfactory employment since aliens were proscribed from most jobs to prevent their taking jobs away from British people. An alternative that was open to the girls was that of nursing.

Merche

Merche also stayed at the Ipswich and Wickham Market colonies. When the small Ipswich colony closed, Merche was sixteen and faced with the choice of going into service or training to be a nurse. She chose the latter course and went to Nottingham to train but the work was not suited to a girl of Merche's squeamish and finicky nature. After working on the wards, she could not bring herself to eat and she lost weight rapidly. At the end of the first month, she weighed six and a half stones. She left Nottingham and went to work as a maid for about six months with a family in Maida Vale. Molly Garratt, who looked after the older boys' interests in London, then found Merche a job as a machinist in a factory and she went to live in the East End.

Fig 13. Taking a break from domestic duties; Merche (2nd from left), Alicia (2nd from right) (Private collection)

Chapter Sixteen

Family Affairs - The Children Grow Up

'My brothers and sisters in Spain had a rough time without either parent. They were earning two or three pesetas a day. The time I had here was a luxury compared with what they had.'

(Valentin)

For as long as the Basque children were minors and in Britain, the National Joint Committee and the Basque Children's Committee held the de facto position of their parents. They were responsible for looking after their health, education and welfare and for keeping track of their actual parents, should the need arise to get into contact with them. Clearly, the most upsetting of such occasions were those involving the death of any of the children. The file held by the Organising Secretary of the Basque Children's Committee recorded nine deaths of children between 1937 and 1943.

A number of the deaths arose from tubercular meningitis, the first to die of this dreadful disease being a young boy aged only seven who was admitted to the Bristol Infirmary from the home in Street and died in the hospital on 26 July 1937. In November, an eight-year-old died of the same disease and was buried temporarily in the Catholic Cemetery in London. The Superintendent of the cemetery was Mr Houchin of Houchin & Son ('the only Catholic Firm of Monumental Sculptors in

London') who was not slow to write to the Basque Children's Committee suggesting that his firm could be of use in erecting a more permanent memorial to the child. The Committee turned the offer down on the grounds that the parents would probably wish at some stage to have the child's body returned to Spain. This awareness of the likely return of bodies led the Committee to follow a standard procedure in cases of death, whereby the body was first embalmed and then buried in a triple-layered coffin, of which one layer was zinc. Until the Civil War was over, the Spanish Embassy in London met the cost of such funeral expenses (from between £25 and £30).

Apart from TB, other causes of death included congestive cardiac failure and acute influenzal pneumonia. One boy drowned at Scarborough in April 1938.

The most worrying case for the Committee was the death of Jose Sobrino at the age of fifteen in the Radcliffe Infirmary, Oxford. The inquest into his death found that Jose had died from delayed arsenical poisoning given as a therapeutic measure for 'congenital specific disease'. The wording of the coroner's verdict was sufficiently low-key to keep any adverse reporting out of the newspapers (the Committee's great concern). The arsenical injections had, in fact, been administered to the boy for treatment of congenital syphilis. He died as a result of this disease, complicated by severe jaundice and sub-acute atrophy of the liver.

It was the task of the Organising Secretary of the Basque Children's Committee to write to parents telling them of the death of their child. Usually, there was enough time to warn the parents that their child was very ill so that the blow of the child's ultimate death was at least to some small extent softened. Such could not be the case if the death arose through an unforeseen accident as in the case of Iñaki, the Scarborough boy. In a touching exchange of letters, Iñaki's parents managed to write a long letter in which they expressed not only their feelings of loss but also their tremendous gratitude for and appreciation of the work carried out on behalf of all the Basque children by the Basque Children's Committee.

No one better exemplified the dedication of those who devoted such a tremendous amount of time and effort to looking after the children's interests than Alice Mabel Picken. She was Secretary to the Basque Children's Committee from the early 1940s through to the 1950s, when the organisation had changed its title to the Basque Trustees and After Care Committee.

Miss Picken conducted a lengthy and fruitful correspondence with the British Consular office in Bilbao, helping to trace missing children and assist in reuniting them with their parents. She also kept up with the children who were repatriated to Spain and France and did her best to look after the interests of children left in Britain who might need the Committee's help. As Ronald Thackrah, Chairman of the Basque Children's Committee in the mid 1940s, said, 'She was held in great affection by all the children who came to her with their problems, and I cannot speak highly enough of her devotion. She did far more than one could expect from a fairly lowly paid, full-time employee of the Committee'.

Once World War II had finished in Europe, a number of parents of children still living in England wanted to renew contact with their offspring. The British Consul in Bilbao found himself acting as a post-box between parents and the Basque Children's Committee office in London, from where Miss Picken chased down the whereabouts of children who could by then have spent more than half their lives in an English-speaking environment and be earning their own living. Typical was a request passed on by the Consul in September 1945 from the parents of Daniel and Valentin Bollada Echevarria who had not heard from or of their two sons since October 1939. Miss Picken duly found out that Daniel was by then articled to a firm of chartered accountants in York and that Valentin was apprenticed to a turbine manufacturer in Newcastle-on-Tyne. The boys' addresses were passed on, via the Consul, to the inquiring parents.

Often, parents only wanted to know how their children were doing and to have some news after several years of silence. A few wanted their children to return but this was not an easy decision for those who had spent the past ten or more years adapting to a British way of life. The mixed emotions and difficulties confronting children in this position were aptly expressed by one who wrote to Miss Picken in 1949. She enclosed a letter from her father in the hope that Miss Picken could get it translated for her (from Spanish into English), 'I should like to see my parents, but I know that I could never be happy in Spain. I should like to settle down in England and marry. But I don't see how that can happen without quarrelling with my people, and I would much rather avoid that. Can you advise me, on what to say?'

Occasionally, the Consul passed on messages to children from parents anxious that they should not return. Such was the case for Julian and Jesus Gonzalez Barredo, whose mother, Isabel, asked the Consul in Bilbao to pass on a message that her sons should not return since they had not returned earlier to Spain to do their military service. They were accordingly regarded as deserters by the Spanish authorities and would be arrested if they set foot in Spain. The parents had been forced to give the address of the younger son to the authorities and it was known that the Spanish Consul in Bilbao would be notified that he was a defaulter. The parents were adamant that the boys should not return and that they should take out British nationality as soon as possible.

Miss Picken handled these cases and many others and her interest in the children clearly went beyond merely dealing with their problems on a nine-till-five basis. She kept detailed lists following the fortunes of the children, whether they had left the country, married, died, or rejoined their families, throughout the 1940s and 1950s. She corresponded at length with at least some of those who returned to Spain and she visited the Basque country from time to time, looking up her former charges and participating in reunions of the children.

One boy, Jose, was deported from England in December 1947. He wrote shortly afterwards to Miss Picken: a terse letter written in spidery block capitals, explaining to her that he had left Vigo for Bilbao where he was now living rather unhappily (he didn't speak any Spanish):

'It was foolish of me to come to Bilbao. I should have stayed in Vigo. The Spanish don't like the English. I don't know why..........There is no privacy in this house............I shall write again, this pen is no good also this letter.

P.S. I am plain stupid or crazy. I don't know, do you?'

Jose also explained in his letter that he had been allowed to bring out only five pounds from England. Although he had not asked for any help, Miss Picken immediately wrote to the Aliens Department at the Home Office to find out how Jose's remaining funds (another five pounds) could be brought out. The Bank of England had given permission for Jose to take his earnings out of the country but, as he was held in Brixton Prison prior to deportation, it had not been possible to get his signature on travellers' cheques. A letter from Messrs Coutts had been given him in the hope that this would suffice as justification for him to take the money out of the country, but, evidently, some official had decided that it was not enough.

Sometimes Miss Picken tracked down children in the nick of time. Ramon de la Cal's father contacted the Consul in Bilbao in 1942 about the whereabouts of his son and Miss Picken found him and passed on the message that the father would like to get in touch. Ramon wrote to Miss Picken in November, enclosing a letter for his father and one for the Consul to thank him for his actions, pointing out that he had written, 'as soon as I could possibly make it due to the fact that I volunteered for the air force this morning.'

As time went on, the number of charges in Miss Picken's capable hands dwindled to a small enough number of children for the Basque Children's Committee to announce in 1949 that, 'our Committee is winding up as practically all the Basque children are now independent.' Before that, however, the Committee had been kept fully occupied during the 1940s, trying to find suitable homes and occupations for well over 400 children. Lists were drawn up in 1941, showing the number and distribution of older girls (those of fourteen years of age and over) and of the younger children under fourteen.

The expressed wish of the Committee was to 'place girls in work or training of real value in after life' but they recognised that many of the girls were educationally unprepared to enter specialised work and that places at technical schools were few and far between. As a consequence, many girls found they had to go into domestic service. Of the 88 girls listed in 1941, 29 were in domestic work and only one was still at school. Five of the older girls had been placed, through friends, in nursing and were reported as 'doing good work and making satisfactory progress'.

Of the other girls, a large number (21) had been found adoptive families and three were in convents. The others were pursuing a variety of trades - dressmaking, tailoring, factory work, gardening and office work. The remaining colonies at Caerleon, Cambridge, Carshalton, Barnet and in Scotland were still financially responsible for some 30 girls.

The working conditions of the Basque girls who found employment were not always ideal. Juanita, who with her sister had been 'rescued' from the convent in Manchester by Dr Duran, left the Duran home after the mother had another child and the accommodation in the flat became too cramped. Juanita's sister refused to go with her to London as she had started to work as a laboratory assistant with the doctor. Juanita was found a place at the Woodside Park colony, having refused to go back to her mother in Spain, who had remarried and had a baby and was living in poor conditions in a one-bedroomed-flat. 'My mother never forgave me - if it had been my father, I'd have gone.'

Aged 15, Juanita was too old to go to school so she went into nursery nursing. After a year she left the colony and the Committee found her a post in Bethnal Green. She stayed at the nursery for three years, working from seven in the morning till seven at night and earning 15 shillings a week. Once a week she went on day release to Kentish Town College as part of her training. By the time she was 18, however, she was feeling very isolated and depressed although she enjoyed the work itself; she became very ill and quit her job. She then turned to tailoring and dressmaking, eventually working for John Lewis.

Although the work had all the boredom of factory work, Juanita began to enjoy herself socially. She was earning more money and used to spend the evenings at the Hogar Español, a social centre for Spanish refugees. She met her future husband, a Catalan, at a dance and once she had had her first child at the age of 25 she gave up working. Originally, Juanita had wanted to train properly as a fashion dressmaker but there were no funds available from the Basque Children's

Committee for such apprenticeships and eventually she gave up such ambitions.

Fig 14. Dancing at El Hogar. (Private collection)

Alicia, on the other hand, wanted to be a beautician and started work in a beauty parlour but found she could not afford it since she was paid nothing. So, as a second best, she started work in a hairdressing salon on Buckingham Palace Road. She worked there for over a year, earning 10 shillings a week. In the end, however, she decided that she was being used rather than being taught. A hairdresser whom she knew, Mrs Laurence, who had a business in Kilburn, was bombed out of her London home and moved to Brighton. Alicia took over the running of the business for her for 30 shillings a week.

Merche worked as a machinist in a factory and lived with a cockney family during the Blitz. Ironically, it had been her great fear of the air raids in Spain that had made her such a willing evacuee in 1937 and, now, she had put herself right in the middle of the worst air raids on London. The first day there were air raids, Merche was at the cinema by herself watching *My Favourite Husband*. 'All the lights went out and everybody was very calm, singing. I kept quiet; I didn't want to make a fool of myself.' However, she felt more than compensated by the independence she had achieved by moving away from the colonies and the inevitable domestic service. During the time that Merche worked in the factory, she earned only just enough to pay for her board and lodgings, so the Basque Children's Committee gave her 2/6d pocket money for several months to supplement her meagre income.

Merche then went to Carshalton for a short period where she was able to train as a secretary at Pitman's, enabling her to obtain employment at the International Commission for Refugees in London. She also applied to the Juan Luis Vives Foundation, an educational trust set up to help pay for training of the Basque children in approved careers, and obtained a grant to study at Croydon Polytechnic. Her ambition was to be a chemist, having always enjoyed maths and being interested in science. But her patchy education since arrival in England and the fact that she was having to catch up on an English rather than a Spanish education made the task seemingly impossible and she gave up after a year.

The Basque children who stayed in Britain went into a variety of careers, ranging from the Merchant Navy to engineering of all kinds, school teaching to secretarial work, nursing to catering. A few very gifted or lucky ones were able to pursue more glamorous ways of earning their living.

Jose Alberdi, whose artistic talent was spotted from a very early age, went on to become a popular and highly successful sculptor whose works included commissions from local authorities, such as Stevenage, and from large City institutions. The Basque Boys in general appear to have been football mad (those lucky enough to live in the small semi in Ipswich found that their back garden faced Ipswich Town's football ground and they were able to watch the home matches for free from the garden wall). Emilio Aldecoa played football for Wolverhampton Wanderers and Coventry City between 1942 and 1947 before leaving England to play for the all-Basque team, Athletic Bilbao. Others who went on to become professional football players included Raimundo Lezama, Jose Gallego and Sabino Barinaga.

Pirmin Trecu's creative bent was evident early on: at the Culvers colony in Carshalton, he formed an Entertainment Committee with two other children. Later on, he became a professional ballet dancer and performed with the Sadlers Wells Ballet in the late forties and early fifties. His name lives on in the Academia de Bailado Classico Pirmin Trecu in Lisbon. Delia, the younger sister of Helvecia, became a dancer and at one time was in the same troupe as a young Audrey Hepburn. Marina de Gabrain became a noted mezzo-soprano who sang in major European opera houses and at Glyndebourne, where she took the eponymous role of *La Cenerentola* in productions in the early 1950s.

Several of the Basque Boys enlisted during World War II and three died in action.

In 1945, just over 400 of the original Basque children were still in Britain but once the war finished a large number left the country, most to Spain but at least seven to South America, the same number to France (presumably to their families who had fled there during the Civil War) and a couple of the girls married Americans and emigrated to the United States. By 1954, 280 children were listed by Miss Picken as still living in Britain, 176 boys and 104 girls. By that time, over half were married and of these marriages at least eight were between Basque children.

Most of the Basque children went back to their families, either in Spain or in France to where so many refugees fled, first from the Basque country as Mola's troops moved closer and later from Catalonia, the last bastion of the Republic's resistance to Franco and his Nationalists. Some Basque children settled permanently in France, married French people and worked in a variety of trades and professions - one worked at the Gruyere factory, another studied to be a teacher and finished as a professor in Australia. Of the ones who returned to their native home, most found jobs eventually and, in some cases, their knowledge of English was a distinct asset in helping them find work with the Customs, for example, or as translators. Many of them were homesick for England for a long time after their return, as testified by the many letters sent to Miss Picken by her former charges.

The 200 or so who remained in Britain were largely those who had only one surviving parent or were orphans. A few had lost touch completely with their family, others had parents who were in hiding or in prison. Unsurprisingly, those who stayed felt to some extent distanced from their families who had been left behind in Spain and now might be in camps in France or living lives of severe economic hardship in Franco's Spain. Girls' relationships with their mothers seem, in particular, to have suffered.

When Juanita was reunited with her mother for the first time, she was a grown young woman with a husband and child of her own. Her mother's background and experiences were totally different from her daughter's and her attempt to reassert her traditional position vis à vis her daughter only led to resentment and misunderstanding. For a village mother it was quite normal to help her daughter take a bath; for the daughter who had been independent and earning her own way since her late teens it was symbolic of the unbridgeable gap between the two of them.

Alicia had similar difficulties with her mother, compounded by considerable resentment at her mother's actions over the years. When still only thirteen or so, Alicia had received a request from her mother, then in a camp in France, to send her some clothes. Sorting through the clothes room in the colony, Alicia selected what she hoped would be a useful parcel of clothing. Her mother wrote back angrily, ticking her off for sending her clothes that were the wrong size. Relations between the two were not helped when the mother stopped corresponding at all because, as Alicia discovered later, she had met a man and was happily involved with him, seemingly forgetting completely her daughter in England. She only got in touch again when the man left her. Eventually, Alicia's mother and younger brother came over to England and stayed a few months with Alicia and her husband and young daughter. The relationship, already strained, reached an almost irretrievably low point at this attempt at renewal.

For others, there were tearful reunions in Spain after many years of exile and regular visits to Spain to visit surviving relatives became common. Valentin first went back to Spain in 1963 and, thereafter, returned almost every year, particularly to watch Athletic Bilbao. Although he recognised the kindness of the English volunteers who had brought the children over, he was bitter about an evacuation that had separated him so completely from the rest of his family, 'I think we should have stayed there. I would be hesitant now, if the same thing happened here, to send away my children or grandchildren....It makes you hard and bitter and you shouldn't be like that should you? If I'd been brought up in a normal household, I would accept.....but I've had to look after myself, grab what you can when you can....I've seen how my family's fared; alright let us suffer together. As a family you benefit by it.'

Valentin is probably an exception; even those who didn't want to be evacuated at the time, such as Luis, recognised that their parents acted in the best interests of their children in sending them away. Luis was, however, one of the lucky ones who was able to pursue his education, gained a degree at Bangor University and went on to become a teacher, marrying a fellow Basque child on the way.

Many of the Basque children who stayed eventually took out British citizenship, if for no other reason than the relative protection afforded by having a British passport. But many were still clearly torn between feeling Spanish or Basque and feeling British. Though they may have lived and worked in Britain, many spent their holidays in Spain, bought second homes there and thought about the possibility of retiring to their native country rather than stay in their adopted one. A few, especially those brought up outside London with its large Spanish-speaking community, no longer spoke any Spanish at all and even answered to anglicised names rather than their given Spanish ones. Others, though they may have spoken English all day, still had to count in Spanish for example.

Fig 15. Niños vascos at the 2010 reunion lunch. Front row, Jose-Pedro 2nd from right; Helvecia 3rd from right; Merche 2nd from right in the second row. (Courtesy Luis Jarero)

So, as with any large group of people, generalisation is dangerous since each Basque child encountered different problems and reacted to situations in a totally individual way as he or she adapted to life in a new country. What does seem to hold true, however, is that the relationships the children forged among themselves in the colonies and afterwards were exceptionally strong, replacing in a sense the relationships they would have enjoyed under different circumstances with the members of their families.

Perhaps the last word should be with Laureana, the young teacher who came over with the children and never returned to Spain to live, although she visited her family there. Her mother wanted her to return but Laureana was too attached to England. 'Freedom is such a big thing,' was Laureana's explanation. She quoted a book, *From Guernica to New York*, 'Freedom was our flesh and blood and that was really true. It's the same today. Freedom of speech and thought.' Laureana had no doubts that bringing the children over had been the right thing to do, 'It's only human to take them...it's safety first...to leave them there to suffer is inhuman.'

Although she recognised that the Basque children had perhaps lived too long in the colonies and certainly missed their parents, she thought that they had been able in large part to preserve their customs just as though they had been at home. As for the English volunteers, 'I don't think we'll ever be grateful enough, thankful enough to these people. Forever in my heart I will be grateful to them. Some of them didn't have all that money...they welcomed us with open arms - which is fantastic isn't it? Well, I think so anyway.'

Source materials and general bibliography

General reading

A number of studies related to the evacuation of the Basque Children (both to the UK and elsewhere) have been published since I first started my researches. Aspects of the topic have also increasingly been the focus of PhD and other theses by academics.

An excellent list of publications can be found here:

http://www.basquechildren.org/reference/bibliography

This site also provides an extensive range of reference materials at:

http://www.basquechildren.org/reference/articles

BasqueChildren.org is the website for BCA '37 UK – The Association for the UK Basque Children. The association was set up in 2002 by Natalia Benjamin and Manuel Moreno, in collaboration with Helvecia Hidalgo, whom I interviewed in the mid 1970s.

Southampton University hosts a significant archive on the Basque children.

Main sources used in this book

Nearly all the information in this book comes from primary sources – contemporaneous documents, including newspapers, letters, telegrams and committee minutes – or from interviews with those involved in bringing over and looking after the Basque children and with a number of the Basque children.

Chapter 1

Report on the visit by an All Party Group of Members of Parliament to Spain, The Press Department of the Spanish Embassy in London, 1936

Chapters 2, 3, 4

The Royal Navy and the Siege of Bilbao, James Cable, Cambridge University Press, 1979

Papers held at the FCO – letters; minutes; telegrams. Documents came from Political Western Spain files: 21302/ 21366/ 21367/ 21368/ 21369/21371.

Chapters 3, 4, 5, 6, 7, 8, 10, 11, 12, 14, 16

Papers given to me by Wilfrid Roberts. These included minutes of meetings of the various committees, including the Basque Children's Committee and the National Joint Committee for Spanish Relief; telegrams sent to and from various members of these committees; correspondence; reports from Stoneham Camp. Warwick University houses a substantial archive of Roberts documents.

Other interviewees, including Ronald Thackrah and Laureana Puerta, also provided certain documents.

Chapters 9, 14, 15 and 16 in particular

Interviews conducted mainly in the mid to late 1970s with helpers, committee members and the Basque children themselves are the primary source of information about the daily routine at the homes and the lives of older children after leaving the colonies.

Issues of *Amistad*, the magazine produced by Basque children and published by the Basque Boys Training Committee

Chapter 13

An extensive interview with Poppy Vulliamy, who welcomed me to stay at her cottage in Diss in the mid 1980s.

A note on illustrations

Where these come from publications, the original is referenced. I have not been able to identify the photographers of the original 1930s photos that are shown. If there are any copyright issues, the author would welcome any information enabling such issues to be resolved for any second edition.

About the author

The daughter of a Basque child evacuee, Yolanda Powell has long been fascinated by why and how Britain took in nearly 4,000 Basque children during the Spanish Civil War. She began working on the story of *The Basque Children in Britain* after graduating from Oxford and continued intermittently with her research while following a varied career in the UK, Europe and the USA. In 2018, she published her first novel *Yellow with Black Spots*, set in the Paris of the 1970s. Her second publication *The Basque Children in Britain* marks the 85th anniversary of the children's evacuation.

www.ingramcontent.com/pod-product-compliance
Lightning Source LLC
LaVergne TN
LVHW011349080426
835511LV00005B/217

* 9 7 8 1 9 9 9 9 2 2 4 2 9 *